ONE
SURRENDERED
A testimony of the power of God displayed in the life of an ordinary man
LIFE

Bob Coy

One Surrendered Life

By Bob Coy, Senior Pastor of Calvary Chapel Fort Lauderdale

Copyright © 2005 by Calvary Chapel Church, Inc.

Requests for information should be addressed to:
Calvary Chapel Church, Inc.
Department of Communications
2401 West Cypress Creek Road
Fort Lauderdale, Florida 33309
Calvary Chapel Church Web site: www.calvaryftl.org

ISBN: 1-932283-25-0

Printed in the United States of America

Dedication

When I considered the dedication of this book, many people came to my mind—my wife, Diane, and my children, Christian and Caitlyn, whom I love dearly; Pastor Chuck Smith, who has influenced me greatly; and even the body of believers and staff at Calvary Chapel Fort Lauderdale, who have blessed me abundantly. But, as I contemplated the content of these pages, there was One who stood out above all the rest. Without Jesus Christ, there would be no story to tell. Without Jesus, I never would have experienced the joy of knowing an extraordinary God who has lovingly transformed me from the inside out. Jesus set the example of what God can do through one surrendered life, and I humbly and gratefully give total acknowledgement to Him.

"For God so loved the world that He gave His only begotten Son, that whoever believes in Him should not perish but have everlasting life. For God did not send His Son into the world to condemn the world, but that the world through Him might be saved."
(John 3:16–17 NKJV)

"For even I, the Son of Man, came here not to be served but to serve others, and to give my life as a ransom for many."
(Matthew 20:28 NLT)

Foreword

When people that are familiar with my husband's ministry first meet me, they typically ask, "Is he this way at home?" I know they are referring to Bob's intensity, his sense of humor, and his relatability that come through his teachings from the pulpit. I can sincerely say the answer to their question is, "Yes." What you see in public is who he is in private. The passion that fuels his teaching is what compels him to spend the same time, energy, and effort on one lost soul at the grocery store as he does on speaking to thousands of people at a stadium event. The childlike and humorous way Bob looks at life is not just inspiration for powerful illustrations; it is how he sees the world around him, and this perspective has made living with him for the last twenty years a great joy. His transparency, although valuable to the ministry, has given us, as a family, the kind of unity that is unbreakable. He is an amazing pastor, but he is an even more amazing father, husband, and man who loves God immensely.

Whenever I hear my husband's testimony, it is hard for me to even imagine that the man described in the beginning of this book is the same man I have been blessed to know and love. The transformation that has taken place in Bob Coy is a testimony to God's faithfulness and one reason why we can all rest in His promise that . . . he who began a good work in you will carry it on to completion until the day of Christ Jesus (Philippians 1:6 NIV). Realizing that we are still a work in progress and yet seeing how radically we have been changed thus far give me confident hope and great anticipation for what God's will holds in the years ahead.

—Diane Coy

Table of Contents

Introduction   1

Chapter One – Wrong Way   8

   Mixed Signals   11

   Cruising Along   18

   The Fast Lane   24

   A Change of Scenery   30

   Impaired Visibility   33

   Bends in the Road   38

   Hitting a Dead End   50

Chapter Two – One Way   62

   Yielding to the Right Way   64

   Power Steering   69

   Driver's Ed   76

   Learner's Permit   92

   The Scenic Route   98

   All-Wheel Drive   110

   The Importance of a Guardrail   117

   Back on Track   128

   The On-Ramp to Ministry   132

Chapter Three – Road Work Ahead 142

Proceeding With Caution 143

Mistaking the Road Signs 152

The Emergency Brake 160

Chapter Four – Keep Right 164

A Matrimonial Merge 165

Traveling Mercies 177

The Exit Ramp 179

Yes, We're There 190

Chapter Five – No U Turn 196

Which Way Do We Turn? 197

Unfamiliar Territory 200

Roadside Assistance 205

The Road Forks 210

Epilogue 220

Introduction

Webster defines "testimony" as "a statement used for the purpose of evidence or proof." When we see in Scripture the expression of a truth and then witness the experience of that truth in a life, there is a validation of God's Word. The testimony of my life is a validation of God's Word on many counts. Through the details of my life, God's saving grace shines forth and assures all who witness that grace that God is in the business of making something out of nothing. My testimony also confirms what God wants to do in all of our lives if we just let Him.

The Bible tells us in Matthew 7:24–25: *"Therefore whoever hears these sayings of Mine, and does them, I will liken him to a wise man who built his house on the rock: and the rain descended, the floods came, and the winds blew and beat on that house; and it did not fall, for it was founded on the rock."*

It continues with a contrast in verse 26: *"But everyone who hears these sayings of Mine, and does not do them, will be like a foolish man who built his house on the sand: and the rain descended, the floods came, and the winds blew and beat on that house; and it fell. And great was its fall. And so it was, when Jesus had ended these sayings, that the people were astonished at His teaching, for He taught them as one having authority, and not as the scribes."*

It is noteworthy that this is Jesus teaching. Who else in all of eternity is a more outstanding authority on the subject of human life? Certainly He would have experiential knowledge of mankind, having witnessed history and having seen how many foolish people chose not to have any spiritual foundation. The result of their foolish, sandy-soiled choices always led to falling, crashing, burning, and destruction.

Yet, in contrast to that, He also watched the wise who would lay for themselves a spiritual foundation based upon His written Word and rather than falling, crashing, and burning, they would become strong, stable, secure, and safe.

The choice of each life path and its final endpoint is set forth in God's Holy Scripture and then becomes a matter of our own personal choice. We can build our house upon rock or sand, but we will encounter the consequences that God says are inherent in each choice.

In many ways my life is a testimony to both sides of this truth. Before coming to Christ, I was on the path of falling, crashing, burning, and destruction. Since coming to Christ, I look back at my new life and clearly see the strong, stable, secure, and safe benefits I have enjoyed from knowing Jesus.

Like so many of you who will read this book, once the

transformation took place I had to get my eyes off the earth and focus them on heaven. I could no longer walk by sight but instead began walking by faith. With the decision to let God be the Lord of my life came an amazing metamorphosis. I am able to look back at the past, learn from it, and reach certain conclusions that I pray, in some way, will assist you wherever you may be on the road of choice right now.

I must give a slight disclaimer as a prelude to this book. This testimony is rated PG-13. The reason for this rating is because I will be sharing a little of my dirt. As hard as it might be for me to tell and as difficult as it might be for some to read about a pastor, I am hoping through the reality of my story to relate to those who may feel that when it comes to God, church, and ministry, they are disqualified because of either their present or past wild lifestyle and immorality.

My prayer is that through the pages of this testimony, you will begin to understand that the only thing that can disqualify any one of us from a relationship with God is our choice to not enter into that relationship at all.

The God who created everything, seen and unseen, and who spans the entire billions of galaxies with His thumb and little finger has a passionate and infinite heart of love for us. His love is so compelling that He has parted seas, shut the mouths of lions, walked on water, calmed storms, fed the hungry, healed the hurting, and ultimately given up His very own life that we might receive a life that is eternal and abundant.

My testimony, like everyone else's who has chosen to build his or her house upon the Rock, displays the divine plan of an Almighty God. When the Lord looked at my life before Jesus, He saw a man meandering upon a broad pathway to hell, who was deceived into thinking he was on the road to success. Graciously, mercifully, and tenderly, God in His sovereignty and providence made sure that His path and mine crossed. This book is the summary of that heavenly orchestration called salvation as it occurred in my life.

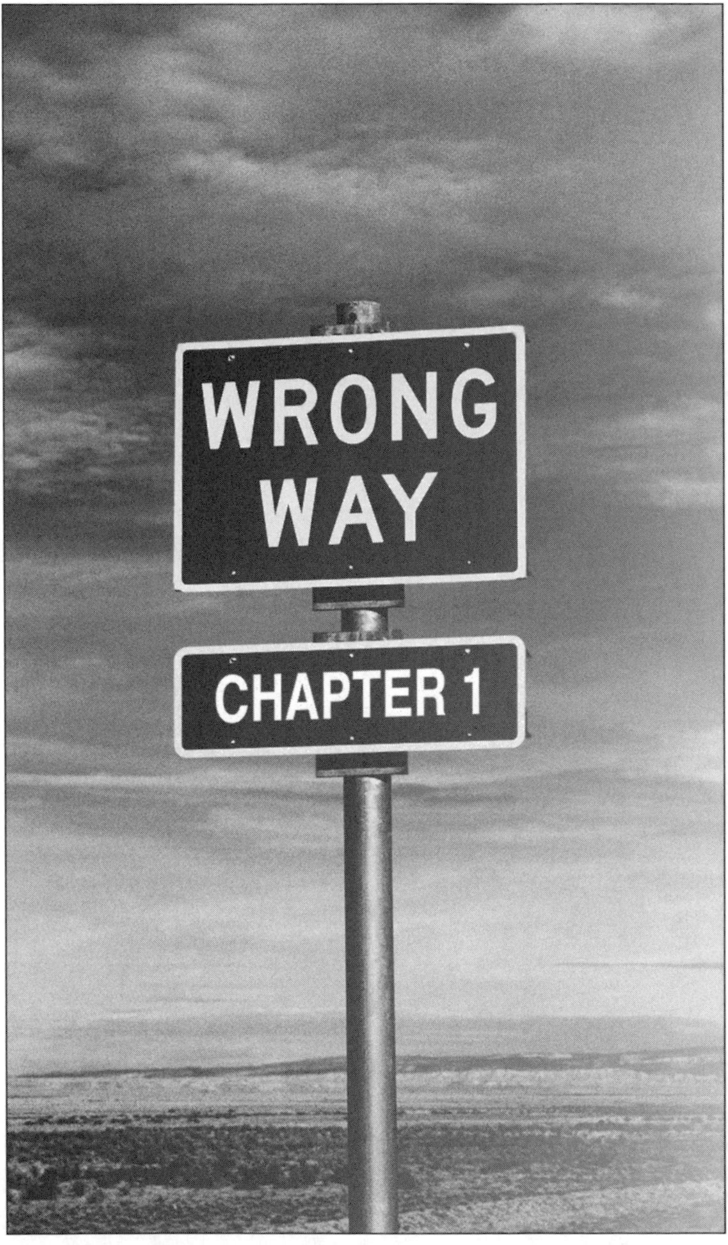
WRONG
WAY
CHAPTER 1

I was raised in the Lutheran church, and as a young boy I could not seem to bridge the gap between what I heard in the Bible and what I saw in practice. As much as I believe that my dad definitely had a sound understanding of what it meant to be a good Lutheran, some of what I experienced growing up confused me. I did not have the basis for understanding God's grace, and what I saw appeared to me to contradict what I heard. My father would zealously teach Sunday school and sing in the choir during the school year, then, when summer came, we didn't go to church. Quite honestly, as a kid, I thought the church closed its doors in the summer. I will never forget seeing cars at the church once dur-

Mom and Dad (Ken and Betty Coy) with my older brother, Chuck, and me.

Chuck

me

My younger brother, Jim, and I dressing up for a school play.

ing the summer and wondering what people were doing there if the pastor was out of town. Now, obviously the pastor was not out of town, but I had assumed that since we didn't go to church during that season, other people didn't go either.

Mixed Signals

Unfortunately, from our pattern of on-again-off-again church attendance, I concluded that there was a lack of commitment in my father's heart about his faith. I know that he loved God because there were many times I can remember sitting as a family and reading the Bible together. But, like all of us, my dad was human. He had his ups and downs, and in my inability to separate his flesh from his spirit, I assumed that there was an inconsistency in his faith.

Now, some thirty years later, as I understand the battle between spirit and flesh, I see things differently.

But it wasn't just from my father's life that I drew mixed signals. I saw the same pattern of flesh versus spirit in the life of our pastor who also happened to be my uncle. As an adult, I have come to discover that there was much more in my uncle's life that, had I been privy to know, would have tipped the scales more on the side of spiritual. Since his death and my conversion, I have found out things about my uncle that convince me that my perspective was skewed because of my young age and lack of understanding of all the facts. Yet, as a young child, what I saw versus what I heard didn't seem to be consistent.

My impressions about my family left me with the conclusion that God probably behaved in the same mixed-signals way—some days He is really gracious, and other days He is very judgmental; some days His compassions never fail, and other times He is ready to beat me over the head with a spiritual billy club. To say the least, my perceptions and the conclusions I drew from them affected my young and impressionable spirit by gravely diminishing my value of spiritual things.

I tell this part of my story not for the purpose of laying blame on my parents or my uncle, but in hopes that any parent reading this book will take note. Perhaps, as you read about the heart of someone who remembers looking at life through the eyes of a child, you can appreciate the adverse effect of growing up without a strong anchor in God's Word. Without any sense of destiny or any spiritual authority, and without any divine awareness of purpose or agenda, I floundered foolishly throughout my childhood and school years.

I became much more a socialite than a student. In fact, I would go so far as to say that I excelled at social activities. Whether it was hanging with a couple of guys in the parking lot or making jokes in class, I loved people. I still do. I can see in hindsight that my love for people has always been a God-given part of my personality—one that I unfortunately used for selfish purposes until I came to know Christ.

I was somewhat of an oddity in that I did not have a specific group that was "my group." I was Captain Schmooze. I would fraternize with all different groups because I genuinely liked everybody. Like a chameleon, I changed myself year after year, depending on which group I was with at the time. One year, I was a greaser—I had the big black boots and slicked my hair back. The next year, I switched to the preppy look. Then another year, I adopted the hippie thing, and when that passed, I took on the grunge look and would do the flannels and the jeans.

I vacillated because of internal mixed signals. I could never figure out who I really was. I didn't have an identity that was based on a solid foundation because I had never gained that foundation growing up, so by the time I graduated from high school, I had become a conglomerate of mixed signals.

We still see this happening in the world today— young people unable to find their identity. They have never been shown what is really important in life, so they have no clue who they are or what really matters.

Like most of my peers, I had not even set goals for myself outside of high school. A few of the rich kids were going to college, but most of us growing up in lower- to middle-income families in Detroit fell back on the fleeting hope of getting a job with one of the really big auto manufacturers.

That meant looking forward to screwing on tail lights eight hours a day for the next thirty years, and, if I didn't get fired, then retiring at around age forty-five, buying a bass boat, and fishing and drinking beer until I died. That did not sound like a lot of fun to me. I began to think, "Man, I have got to get out of here" and, oddly enough, that became my goal—to break out. I wanted to do something with my life, and I believed, quite honestly, that I could.

We will all look back one day to our high school graduation pictures and ask, "What was I thinking?"

Cruising Along

My early ambition was to be a millionaire before age twenty-one, and I didn't hesitate to tell people that. I had a cocky kind of confidence and the audacity to believe that I could really do it. I saw sales as an avenue to accomplish my dream. The scary thing was that I really could. My people skills made me a natural in the sales world.

When I got out of high school, one of the first jobs I landed was in the sales department at a record store. People would come in and tell me what they liked, and I would help them pick out something. Over time, they trusted my judgment because I seemed to have an innate sense of what was really good music.

Even though I was young, I saw the potential to make money in the record business. I knew what people liked, what they bought, and what products sold the best. As I pondered the prospect, I realized that the guys who were making the records were actually the ones with the big bucks.

About that time, the manager of the store came to me and said, "Bob, I'm watching you. For some reason, you seem to know what is happening musically even before we are able to buy it. Why don't you listen to some stuff and tell me what you think?" So I did. He started buying according to what I liked, and before I knew it he made me the buyer for that store.

In the short period of time I was there, our little store in Detroit went from the lowest-sales store to the highest because I kept picking hits. I didn't even know I had it in me, but I liked it a lot. I loved listening to music and being in the know about what was hot and what was not.

I built a reputation for myself among the small chain of record stores in that area. Next thing I knew, someone showed up at the department store where I was working and said, "Hey, you've got a reputation for picking good music, and I'm ready to open up a twelve-store chain. How would you like to work for me picking out my music?"

So, there I was, not yet twenty, picking out music for this guy who was building twelve record stores in Detroit. I had a decent car, a nice apartment, and, in my mind, I was on that road to my first million. I was starting to do something with my life.

While working in retail, I got this idea that there

might be more money in wholesale. About the same time, someone from United Artists came knocking on my door and offered me a job selling records to retail stores. I had advanced one more notch toward my goal when I began working for United Artists.

I stayed with them for nearly a year when there was another knock on the door from someone in the business. "Hey, Bob, I don't know if you know this, but Capitol Records is going to buy out United Artists. They are going to dump most of their sales reps, but we would like you to stay on. You know how to pick a hit."

Incredible! I was twenty-one years old, and I had landed a job with a major record label, which was not an easy thing to do. It was a job most people my age would have died for. I had a sports car, a company car, an apartment in one of the finest gated communities in Detroit, and a good income—and the perks didn't stop there.

When I went to a bar, I could introduce myself as, "Hi, I'm Bob Coy, Capitol Records." If that doesn't help your head swell, nothing will! And when people would ask me what I did for Capitol Records, I'd make sure they knew that part of my job description was hanging out with rock stars. I could get tickets to any concert. What an in!

I was the liaison between the rock stars that came to Detroit and the record company in Hollywood. So, for all the rock stars that visited Detroit, I was the guy picking them up at the airport, taking them where they were supposed to go, and making sure that while they were in my city, they were happy—at whatever expense.

This is the epitome
of ~~"Bob Coy~~
Capitol Records."
Here I am schmoozing with
some of the rock stars.

The Fast Lane

I was twenty-one, a heathen, living by mixed signals, and thinking that I had died and gone to heaven. I was into drugs, alcohol, and women—all without limit. This was the point in my life when I was introduced to cocaine.

I will never forget the first time. The vice president in charge of marketing turned to me and said, "Hey, Bob, do you want to, uh," with gestures I misinterpreted for eating. "Sure, I'd love to, I'm starving." To my shock, he broke out a bag of cocaine and set out lines for us. Not wanting to disappoint my boss, I took the first hit of what I came to think was going to be my ticket home.

In those days, we were under the false notion that

cocaine was the one drug you could not get addicted to. We had to be the most gullible and stupid generation to believe that one, but, in my ignorance, I did believe it, and I became very addicted to cocaine.

There is a truth in this you cannot afford to miss. Just because you are sincere in your belief, if you are wrong, your sincerity will not clear you from the consequences. I sincerely believed that cocaine was not addicting, but I was sincerely wrong, and I suffered the hard and cruel reality of my mistaken assumption without any grace afforded to me for my heartfelt convictions.

Now, as anyone who has used cocaine knows, you have to wash it down with something. That's when I started abusing alcohol. I had a bar in my apartment, and I would wake up and immediately have to have a drink because I was so wiped out from the night before. From experience I knew that I could either feel hung over all day or have a drink and get right back into the swing of things. The fact that I had to start drinking from the moment I woke up in the morning should have been a serious wake-up call. Instead, it became a vicious cycle that hastened my rapid downward spiral.

It didn't take long for the destruction that accompanies such a lifestyle to take its course. The star of the office suddenly became the fool of the office. My addictions began to take control. Instead of me using alcohol and cocaine, they were using me. The same boss who two and half years earlier had said, "I wish I had five guys like you in my office. I want to clone you," now turned to me and said, "Bob,

I'm going to have to can you if you don't get a grip on your life."

The most horrific part of this was that I could not even see what he was talking about. I actually was clueless enough to ask, "What? What do you mean?" He then proceeded to recount for me all the buffoon behavior of which I had been guilty: "Well first, Bob, you lost the keys to the Capitol Records Building. Also, you have been drinking and driving so much, you lost your driver's license. You can't drive in the State of Michigan." He continued to list irrational and irresponsible behavior that had caused him to question my ability to perform my job. I was listening and thinking, "Yeah, that wasn't very good—especially the losing-the-keys-to-the-building part."

I had become so engrossed in my addictions I

could not think straight. I did, however, remember the night I had lost the keys. I was at a party with a bunch of disc jockeys and other popular people and someone said, "Hey, do you want to dance?" I grabbed the keys out of my pocket and threw them down, and I just started dancing like a fool. I'm sure someone must have said, "Hey, that's Bob, he works for Capitol Records, and those are the keys to the building. Let's grab them." The problem was, I just wasn't thinking at that time.

That's exactly what your idol, drug, or vice will do to you. Whatever it is, it is going to take you to a point where you are not thinking straight anymore, and you won't even realize it until you find yourself, like I did, with your boss in your face saying, "Hey, if you don't get a grip, you're going to have to say goodbye."

I took stock of the situation and knew I was on my last leg at the job. I thought, "I am going to have to clean myself up." That's what we tend to do when we get confronted by the aftermath of a destructive lifestyle. We think, "I'll clean myself up." I found out soon enough that this thought process was as destructive and futile as my drug and alcohol-induced mindset.

I was contemplating how to get my life straightened out when I met a girl who was into numerology. In an effort to "clean myself up," I had her tell me my numbers and do a little chart. When that didn't work, I met another girl who was into New Age. That didn't work, either. Then I met another girl who gave me some Mantras that we chanted. I remember kneeling with her in that funny position that makes your thighs hurt the next day and chanting.

I was trying to heal myself from alcohol and drug addiction, but it wasn't working. My boss got painfully honest with me and said, "Goodbye, Bob." No more rock and roll. No more wild lifestyle. No more Bob Coy, Capitol Records.

A Change of Scenery

I had made a few friends who were doctors when I was at the top of the ladder. One of them had moved his practice to Las Vegas. He wasn't really into the medical side of his practice but had a great brain for business and started to buy up property. He needed somebody to manage his properties, so I told him I would move out to Vegas and take that position.

He took me up on the offer, and I was pretty happy for a while, until I started hearing that little voice say, "You're not happy working for somebody else! Come on. Be free. Millionaire by twenty-one, remember? You're missing it, Bob." I began to want to get back on the corporate ladder. I started thinking in terms of a promotional position, and since I still had connections at Capitol Records, I knocked on some casino doors and said, "Hey, I can get country western artists in here through some people I know at United Artists." They agreed, and I became an independent contractor, booking bands up and down the Las Vegas strip until it culminated in a job as an entertainment director at one casino. It was great money, and I found myself living the "good life" again, this time in Las Vegas.

There was something happening in my heart, though, that had started at Capitol Records when I was hanging out with some very wealthy young people. I could tell they were not really happy with their lives. I will never forget one conversation I had with a rock and roll star in the back seat of a limousine. He said, "Bob, here's what I can't figure out. Do people really like me for me? Or do they like me only because of who I am as a rock star?"

That was not at all what I had envisioned life would be like at the top. Instead of having all the answers and being ecstatic, he was lost, miserable, and lonely—and he was not a solo case. Many of the stars I encountered were in his same boat. I remember being struck as if by a bolt of lightning with the realization that money and success do not equal happiness and contentment.

What a rude awakening that had been back then,

and yet now I found myself in the midst of the Las Vegas scene with hundreds of people flocking to the casinos, where life is supposed to be one big party, and it was the same truth. It was like déjà vu in the back seat of that limousine. It was that same black hole of despair.

I watched people come into the casinos with lots of money, trying to find happiness by getting more money. The strange thing was that if they won money, they still weren't happy. And if they lost money, they would get mad. It was a no-win situation. I had the thought, "This is nuts."

Impaired Visibility

When I was the entertainment director at this one casino, I thought I would try some new things in one of the lounges. I tried the urban cowboy thing with the electronic bull, but the insurance skyrocketed, and we had to look for an alternative plan.

As we were kicking around some other ideas, my boss suggested we try an all-girl revue. "What do you mean?" I asked. "You know, like girls. No clothes. The whole thing. The girlie show," he answered. I said in almost uncontrollable amazement, "Me manage a naked-girl show? Like, I would hire the girls?"

Please picture the magnitude of the moment. I am a young guy with absolutely no spiritual backbone in me at all, so I am thinking, "I have just hit the Lotto! You bet I'll do this." So, I did.

Part of the marketing strategy for that particular casino was to have one of the local magazines run an article on new shows. As embarrassing as it is for me to admit this, there was an article written on this new girl revue with a picture of me on the cover of the magazine, standing in front of the casino with my hand lifted up to the marquee.

Right now, you need to know that as I thought about what I would share in this testimony, I really wanted to leave out just about everything I have told you up to this point, but the Lord would not let me. Although many people who read this have never been addicted to cocaine, worked at a major record company, or managed a casino with an all-nude revue, there will be many who have done things they feel are equally abominable in the eyes of God, and they need to know that there is victory available beyond that point. God can redeem even the vilest of sins.

As I considered that I might be risking my

reputation as a pastor by putting down these horrific details of my life, God reminded me that I don't have a reputation to risk. All the holiness or righteousness that anyone might see in me as Pastor Bob belongs totally and completely to God. I am His workmanship created in Christ Jesus for good works that I simply walk in (Ephesians 2:10). None of it belongs to me. What does belong to me, I am too ashamed to claim.

I am continually baffled at how many people think that pastors are so holy that they would never think or do anything human. They really believe that we don't struggle. Can I dismantle that myth? I am as human as any man that ever walked this earth, and I struggle like anyone reading this book right now. I have had the same temptations as you. One thing, however, that I do have that others may not is that

God allowed me to taste a bit of almost everything that the world has to offer and to find out that there is no real happiness in any of it. I had to come to that place in life where I had exhausted myself in the world of drugs, alcohol, and everything that goes with them before I could comprehend the futility of finding my significance in any of them. Whether it was the pride of having all my buddies come down to the casino where I was in charge and knew all the girls, or whatever it may have been, I came to the place where I realized it was all counterfeit and I was starving for something real.

I have told you these things so that you can see the reality of what God can do with someone who is ready to give up the old self. Some of you may be thinking at this point that if God can use a wretched man like me to accomplish Kingdom business, then you are definitely in the running for a place in His plan. If you're thinking that, you're right, and you're ready to read on.

Bends in the Road

My story gets worse. I was in front of the casino one night and pretty bothered about my life because I had tasted enough of what it was to do right to know that there must be something better than what I was experiencing.

I was convinced that deep down everyone would like to live the Christian life. I just believed that a lot of people would rather live that life without Jesus. Everyone would like to feel peace and joy. Everyone would like to display all the fruit of the Spirit. But not everyone wanted to have to go to God to get that kind of life.

I began to think that whatever happiness I had experienced in a bottle or a relationship was only temporal. It was foolish and fleeting, and it wasn't real joy. I even wondered if there was such a thing as real joy. I started thinking about God again.

Around that same time, my brother, Jim, called me. He had been in California, and from the conversation I discovered that he had been "born again." My reaction was anything but positive. "What did you do? What? Come on, Jim. We were raised in the same home. We both saw our uncle mix the drinks. . . ." He was persistent, "No, Bob, it's different. I don't have a religion. I have a relationship with Jesus Christ." I thought, "Oh wonderful. This is going to be

Jim and Theresa Coy
back in the vegas days.

great. We'll probably have a great time if he moves to Las Vegas." In spite of my skepticism, one thing led to another, and I was making arrangements for Jim and his wife to move to Vegas.

I wasn't prepared for what happened next. It was like that old movie, *Invasion of the Body Snatchers*, only reversed. This was not the same brother I remembered. I know he said he got religion, but it didn't take long for me to decide that he had gotten something much, much more. I knew a lot of religious people, but I had never met anyone like this. He really loved his wife and cared about his family to a point that I had never seen before in anyone else. I thought, "Something is happening here." In fact, it was such a sweet love, I had a hard time believing it was real. It made me want to gag. "Stop it!" I thought. "Don't love her like that." He was always holding her hand or putting his arm around her shoulder. "Stop it. What are you doing?" Whenever I did question him about it, he would say that he loved her like that because of Jesus.

As much as I scoffed outwardly, I longed inwardly for what he had. I could see that he definitely had something I didn't. One night, while I was sitting in front of the casino, I began to wonder. All the lights were on, and I was watching the SAHARA sign flashing back and forth. I don't know why, but I said a prayer.

Most people know how to do that. They may not go to church or read the Bible; they may believe verses that aren't in the Bible, like "God helps those who help themselves," but in times of turmoil, they pray. The problem is that their concept of God is so off that they typically offer their prayer to the "Man Upstairs" or some other bizarre idea or image of God. Just as a side note, from this present point in my life after more than twenty years of discovering who God really is, I find this reference to God somewhat comical. Why do we think He is upstairs? Is it like we rent out a room to God? In light of what I know now of God's awesome majesty and power, calling Him the "Man Upstairs" is ludicrous.

It wasn't comical then, however, so I lifted up a prayer to the "Man Upstairs." "Hey, God. You know I am not happy. Listen, if You bring me a wife, I'll do it right." I prayed that prayer, and wouldn't you know, that night one of the dancers said to me, "Bob, I look in your eyes, and I see you are not real happy. I've got a relative that is coming to town. I bet you two would hit it off." I said, "Really? What's her name?" I could not believe my ears. Her last name was Sunday. Sunday? And I thought, "Is that You, Lord? Are you sending me a girl named Sunday so that I can know it is from You?"

She arrived in town, and we met. She worked for an airline and was a very attractive girl. I was thinking, "This may work." In the car, she said to me, "Do you believe in providence?" "Providence?" I stammered. She continued, "Well, do you know that God can work out circumstances?" "Yeah, sure I do," I said. Then she said the most incredible thing. "I think you are supposed to marry me." "You do?" "Yes," she said. "All you have to do is be born again." Then I said, "Born again? What are you talking about?" She explained, "Well, I'm born again, and anyone I marry has to be born again."

I need to stop here and let you in on another critical piece of this puzzle. While she was saying that she was born again and that I needed to be born again, she was still snorting my cocaine, drinking my beer, and using the foul language I was used to. That made me start thinking, "Well, I don't know if I can be born again like my brother, but I can sure be born again like this girl. Yeah, I can do this."

So, I said a prayer with her to be born again, and twenty-four hours later I was pledging my life to this girl at a Las Vegas chapel. We moved so quickly that my brother, Jim, and his wife, Theresa, were the only ones who made it down to the chapel that night. They stood next to us with their eyes rolling like, "What is he doing now?"

Las Vegas BLVD
800
STOP
Cupid
WEDDING
CHAPEL
I don't think it's a coincidence that «Cupid» rhymes with «stupid».

In hindsight, I can't blame them. I called him and said, "Jim, I found a girl. She'd meet your approval. She's born again. Come on. Meet me down at the chapel. We're getting married." I am still amazed at the amount of composure he mustered up when he said, "Bob, you've only known her three days."

Anyone who has a younger brother will relate to my response, "Jim, listen. I'm your older brother. Get off my back. Something good is happening in my life. Why do you always have to put me down?" Reluctantly, Jim replied, "Okay, we'll be there." And sure enough he and Theresa showed up, and as they were standing there I was thinking, "What did I get them into? They must think I have lost my mind."

It probably goes without saying, but let me say it anyway—when you make fleshly, carnal decisions, I don't care how much you spiritualize them, if they are not based upon the Word of God and birthed from His will, they won't last. And that decision to get married, although it didn't last longer than three weeks, got further than my decision for Christ, which never even got off the ground.

My new wife had to fly back to Pittsburgh after our wedding. I was supposed to go meet her parents and then bring her back to Vegas. In that three-week period of time that she was gone, I got an apartment and furnished it, bought her a car, and made everything ready for her return. Then, I flew to Pittsburgh, and she met me at the airport.

You can imagine my devastation when she said, "I'm not sure." I said, "You're not sure about what?" to which she replied, "Well, there's this other guy." Not even believing my ears, I said, "Well, I got an apartment, I got a car, we made some plans, we have furniture, we picked out colors, and we're married, you know." She stood her ground, "Well, I'm just not sure."

I went ahead and met her parents anyway, but later on the way to meet my parents, we decided that we were not going to stay together. So, I introduced her to my parents as the girl I was going to marry. We went back to her parents and told them it was off.

As I was flying back to Vegas, I looked out the plane window, stared up in the sky, and said, "Oh, so this is the kind of girl You bring to a guy like me. Thanks a lot, God, this is great. What is this, a trick in heaven? If that's the way You operate, forget it."

Have you ever been disappointed by God? Have you ever been at a place where you didn't know what

He was doing because you couldn't see the big plan? At a moment like that, you can be disappointed because in your own wisdom and based on your own understanding, you cannot fathom how any good could ever come of the situation. It is in moments like these that we turn our back on the Lord. And that's exactly what I did.

Hitting a Dead End

I went back to Las Vegas and decided not only was I not born again, but I wasn't even going to be a moral person any longer. Up to that point, I had my limits. Although I had gotten mixed signals in my childhood, those signals actually stemmed from the basic concept of right and wrong that had been embedded in me by my Lutheran upbringing.

Just to clarify—especially if you are a Lutheran or have had a Lutheran background—it is not my intention to paint the Lutheran church with a broad brush. I'm just saying that my experience was not a good one. I think that the church just seemed so traditional and denominational that as a young child I never made the connection I needed to make for God to be real to me. I don't know if I just missed it, but I don't remember hearing, even after all the years of attending church, that Jesus had a plan for my life. Maybe it was said, but I didn't hear it.

I'm not using this as a justification for what I did, but I am letting you see why, on my way back to Vegas, I basically decided to chuck anything that was even remotely spiritual. I figured I'd go for the gusto and enjoy life to the maximum. I started sinning from that point forward like I'd never sinned before.

I didn't find this out until after the fact, but about that time Jim and Theresa were watching my life carefully. They had seen what happened with my "wife," and they were growing more and more concerned about my new course of destructive behavior. Jim and Theresa told me later that when I fell to such new depths of depravity, they almost gave up hope. One of them actually said, "Let's start praying for somebody else. Evidently, God's not answering our prayers for Bob." The other one said, "Yeah, I think he's going to be a heathen until he's dead." Finally, one of them said, "No, we can't be walking by sight. We've got to walk by faith. Let's keep on praying for Bob."

Can I tell you that I am so glad they did?

I'm not really sure if my younger brother realized

at the time what a profound effect his walk with God had on my life. I grew up with this guy, and he made my life look vanilla. He was the real wild man! You know how some people get themselves in trouble, but they know how to land on their feet? Not Jim! Jim would do something really weird or really wild, and then he'd be stuck there. And I'd get a phone call, "Hey, guess what? I'm in jail. Don't tell Mom and Dad. Listen, I need three grand. Get over here." "Three grand? What did you do?" and I'd go bail him out.

Jim lived in reckless abandon. He didn't care about anything. For this guy to change and suddenly be a faithful, loving family man who adored his wife and God and was going to church truly made me stop and take notice. "What happened to you?" was all I kept thinking.

But now, I had this thing in the back of my mind about being born again. I knew I didn't want religion, but this seemed to be something so different. I loved the things I saw in Jim's life, even if I wasn't really sure about the whole God thing. Then, when I met my first wife, and she claimed to be born again too, it was confusing because her life didn't seem like Jim's. Yet, I was willing to take the chance until I thought God had disappointed me, and then I stubbornly set my heart and course on a path to sin so wantonly that sin started to get the better of me.

I lived in this duality for what seemed like eternity. I was having wild parties, but I would go right back to the apartment where I was living and just sit there. From my window, I could see the SAHARA sign on the corner of the Las Vegas strip. I would watch it every night, and as each letter blinked one after the other until it spelled out the word "S-A-H-A-R-A." I even remember the dumbest details like the display that registered the outside temperature and time. I would watch that sign all night long, alone in my room, and I would be so empty I would cry. I was thinking things like, "I don't get it. I'm afraid of life." Outwardly, my life still looked great. I had a little Fiat X19. I had a quarter gram of cocaine in my pocket at all times. I had Kool and the Gang in the tape deck. I was dating Miss Legs Nevada. Yet, inwardly, I was empty, tired, and defeated. I knew I was killing myself, but I didn't know how to stop it. I can remember drinking a Heineken and thinking, "I don't even want to drink anymore. I don't want to do drugs, but I can't do anything else because life doesn't have anything

SAHARA

MAGIC to the EXTREME

STEVE HAYRICK

In hindsight, it was quite apropos that I would be staring at the name of a desert when inside I felt like a dry wasteland myself.

else to offer. This stinks!" Maybe you've been there. Maybe you're there now.

This whole time, Jim and Theresa kept praying. It was December 1980 when my brother called me and said, "Hey, what are you doing for Christmas?" I said, "Well, I'm going to have a party at the casino on Christmas Eve, and I don't know what I'm doing the next day." He said, "Why don't you come over to my house and open up gifts with us? I know Theresa and I would love to see you, and your niece, Melissa, would love to have her uncle at the house for Christmas." Sarcastically, I responded with something like, "Oh, yeah, well, that'll be a great time, Jim, spending the day with you and the family. Wow, can't think of a more swinging thing to do." Jim simply and graciously just reiterated the offer and let it go at that.

I think that is why I accepted the invitation and told him I would be there in the morning.

I had the big party the night before with all the dancers, slot guys, pit bosses, and card dealers. We got so wasted that I didn't wake up the next day until three o'clock in the afternoon. I totally blew off Jim and his family for the morning of opening presents. I felt horrible on the inside. I called him and said, "Hey, I'm on my way over. I'm sorry I'm late." I stopped at a store to pick up a bottle of something. I showed up at their door and cavalierly said, "Hey, man. What's going on? I brought you this bottle of booze."

I don't think I'll ever forget the look on Theresa's face as she stood there. It wasn't a look of judgment or condemnation or even criticism. She just looked at my face and tears began to roll down her cheeks. I said,

"Hey, what are you crying about?" With words that cut like a knife she said, "Bobby, I know that God has so much more for you, and I believe you know it, too. That's all. Come on in." Jim looked at me and, again, I didn't see disgust or disappointment, I just saw frustration. I never felt judged around them. I never felt like they thought I was a horrible person. I just felt their pity, and I have to tell you that their compassion and concern accomplished more than any sermon they might have preached ever could have.

We gathered around the table for dinner, and I felt sick emotionally and physically. I tried to eat, but my stomach wasn't really in the mood for food because of what I had put it through the night before. I started feeling a little nauseous, and I think my face must have been a dead giveaway because Jim turned to me and said, "Hey, you don't look so good. I don't think you should drive back home. Why don't you just stay here for the night?" With that, he tossed me a pillow and blanket.

Wrong Way

Just before he went to sleep that night, Jim grabbed a Bible and gave it to me. He really didn't have to make an effort since he had Bibles everywhere in his house. There was one in the bathroom, the kitchen, and each bedroom. He probably had them in his closets, too. He had a little New Testament, a little Old Testament, a big family Bible, a big, big coffee-table Bible, and then one so big you could use it for a coffee table! You could serve a meal on that Bible! No, I'm just joking, but I'm serious about the fact that he had Bibles everywhere.

So, he handed me a Bible and said, "Hey, why don't you read something good for you before you go to bed?" So, I took the Bible and muttered, "Oh, okay." I really had no intention of reading it, but it was a unique thought, and it really got me thinking about the fact that this was the Holy Book and my life was so unholy.

Yielding to the Right Way

Do you ever have those times when you're just thinking? Thoughts are coming and going along with the hours, but you are so lost in the process itself that you don't even realize how much time has actually passed? I must have been thinking for a couple of hours when I finally opened the Bible. I don't even know what led me to open it, but I did, and I began to read.

I had heard somewhere along the way that if you are going to read the Bible, a good place to start is the Gospel of John, so I turned there and started reading.

I started in the first chapter of John and read all the way through to John 3:16: *For God so loved the world that He gave His only begotten Son, that whoever believes in Him should not perish but have everlasting life (NKJV).*

That's a passage with which I think many of us are familiar. But the clincher for me came in verse 17: *For God did not send His Son into the world to condemn the world, but that the world through Him might be saved (NKJV).*

At this point, my emotions got the better of me. I started thinking, "Wait a minute! He didn't send His Son in the world to *condemn* the world but to *save* it. Condemn—Save—Condemn—Save." The words reverberated in my heart, and I thought, "Saved? That's what I need. I need to get saved. I need salvation. I need to get this thing out of my heart. I need to be set free. Jesus is not going to condemn me."

I had always thought that God was mad at me. I thought He was a God of anger and wrath. I didn't know He is a God of compassion and grace. I realized that what I needed more than anything else in the entire world was God. I needed to be born again—for real.

Here's where the story takes on an even more supernatural note. Just as I was beginning to break, just as my head was comprehending for the very first time the message of the cross in a way that brought tears to my eyes, and just as my heart was responding to the gospel, who do you think showed up in the living room but my brother and his wife. They came out of the back bedroom with Jim leading Theresa by the hand. He asked me, "Hey, what are you doing?" I said,

"I'm reading the Bible. And I just read something I can't believe." Then he said, "Well, God just woke me up and told me to come out here and pray with you to receive His Son." I heard myself saying, "Well, I think He wants you to do that. I think I want to do that."

Now, Theresa, who knows me really well said, "Bob, you know this means God wants to turn your life around 180 degrees? That would mean a complete change." I knew what she was really saying was, "I want to see you change, man! We're not just going to pray a meaningless prayer here, buddy!" I think it was the first time I actually registered the truth of what I said next, "Oh, no. I do want to change. I want to change 100 percent. I want to change all the way around." As if she just couldn't believe her ears, she reiterated the challenge, "Okay, but I'm telling you right now that Christianity is a change of life. It's a change. Do you understand that it is a change?" I knew she had to be thinking about my past life up to that point, so I assured her, "Yeah, I want to change. I really, really want to change."

Jim jumped in at this point and said, "Then get on your knees. Pray this prayer with me." He put his arm around me and prayed a prayer like the one I've prayed hundreds of times at Calvary Chapel Fort Lauderdale: "Lord God, I open my heart, and I invite You inside, to be my Savior, to be my God, and to be my Friend. Forgive me of my sins."

I was following along in the prayer, but when I said, "Forgive me of my sins," it was like heaven opened and suddenly God's grace was lifting off the burdens of alcohol, cocaine, and womanizing. All this stuff just started to lift, and I felt really, really light. It was weird and good all at the same time. Tears were flowing down my face because I could feel the love and forgiveness of God, but the thing that I remember the most was that I felt so light. It was as if I was walking on air or something.

At that point, I knew God had come into my heart and that a transformation had taken place. I was saved, and I knew it. I even said to my brother, "Jim, I think I'm saved." He looked at my face and said, "There's no doubt you're saved. You're really saved."

Power Steering

That night in my brother's living room was my Mount of Transfiguration experience, but the next day, just like the disciples with Jesus in Matthew 17:9,

Now a gift and souvenir shop,
this is the site of the casino
where I used to work
The lights are the same,
but the only thing that resembles
the inside I knew is my memories.

I had to go down the mountain into the valley where the devil was waiting for me at the casino.

On my way to work, I was amazed at the joy of God that was welling up within me over the most basic things of life. I don't think I had ever really seen the sky before that day, or at least it never looked so beautiful to me. I was also seeing trees in a whole new way. I slowed down to look at a blade of grass and was wowed by it. I was enjoying God's creation and communing with Him through it. I remember I prayed on the way to the casino, "God, thank You so much for salvation. Thank You for this feeling of being so light. Wow, God, I really like what You did with that cloud over there. You truly have something going on with nature here. You've got this thing really dialed in, don't You?!" I was just having the greatest time in my newfound relationship with God when suddenly the world was upon me—I had arrived at the casino.

Entering the casino that day was an eye-opening experience. Sin had so blinded my eyes to the truth about life that I had never realized the darkness of depravity in which I had been living. As I went from my car, where I had been wowed by the beauty of the sky to the point of worship, into my place of work, it was as if I walked out of heaven into hell. There I was in the pit of iniquity when one of the dancers walked up to me and said, "Hi, Bob."

I think it may have been the sudden realization of how dark that place really was that made me turn to one of the girls and exclaim, "You know what happened last night?" She said, "No telling. You look very strange." And I said, "Well, here's what happened.

I asked Jesus into my life." In complete shock, she said, "You did what?" It took no time at all for the buzz to spread like wildfire to all the people working in the casino. "Bob got religion! Bob got religion!"

The reactions were interesting. One girl said, "Oh, I can't believe this! Oh, please! This is a phase. You can't be one of them! Don't do this to me, Bob! I need you here!" I thought, "Wait a minute. You need me to keep on sinning so that we stay on the path to hell? That's what you need me to do for you? Oh no!" It was truly disheartening to realize that I had been helping other people stay in darkness and go to hell.

Another girl had a very different reaction. She said, "Ah, this is so cool! You're like a . . . you're like changed. You're different. Are you still attracted to me?" I had not even thought about that, but when I did, it dawned on me that I did have a strong feeling toward her, but not like I used to. I had a strange and deep burden for her soul but not her body. It was very surreal.

The various comments I heard from everyone made me realize that, just like me prior to getting saved, people in general don't have a clue what it means to be born again. Salvation is not a topic they have studied, and so they have no idea what it means to get saved. What's worse is they don't even realize they need it. I got so many mixed reactions on my salvation experience that I knew I needed to know God's Word so that I could supply answers. I remember thinking, "I have to get into the Bible to find answers for all these lost people."

I wasn't sure what to say to most of my co-workers.

I just answered, "Well, I don't know how. All I can tell you is I got on my knees, asked Jesus into my heart, and now I'm different. I don't want to work here anymore. That's all I know."

Driver's Ed

Jim could see that I was struggling about my job. It was the second week after I got saved when I told him, "I cannot go back there. I just sit in my office all day. I can't even go out into the casino. I don't want to talk to any of the people there that used to be my friends because they all think I've lost my mind. I don't have a desire to hang around that place anymore. My buddies are calling me to go out and party, but I just don't have the desire to do those kinds of things anymore." He said, "Well, what do you want to do?" I said, "I don't know. I guess I've got to find another job. It's going to be hard, though, because my car is a company car. If I say goodbye to the job, what am I going to do for wheels? My apartment is even provided by the casino. When I say goodbye to my job, I say goodbye to my place to live as well."

At that point, Jim turned to me and said, "Theresa and I have been praying. Why don't you come live with us?" I said, "You mean it?" He replied, "Yeah, come on and live with us." I knew that he and Theresa were making this offer out of the kindness of their hearts, and I hated to impose on them, but I was desperate to get out of the darkness of my old lifestyle, so I jumped on the offer.

Soon after I moved in, Jim told me, "Hey, Bob. You know, now that you're living here, you can join us in our nightly Bible studies." I said, "You have nightly Bible studies?" He said, "Oh yeah. Every night we have a study." I found out later that these "nightly Bible studies" started the night I moved in. He did this just for me because he knew how much I needed to know the Word.

I said, "What are you studying?" Wisely, he chose, "Well, we're studying the book of Romans." "You are?" I asked. "Ah, yeah, Romans. In fact, tonight we're in Chapter One, verse one," he answered.

What Jim and Theresa did for me was one of the best things that could happen to a brand-new believer. They made their house an accepting haven for a sinner saved by grace. They provided all that I really needed, which was the Word of God and people who loved me enough to bear with me during those years of being a baby Christian.

I bring this up because sometimes as believers we can have the mindset that says, "I did my job. I brought my friend to church, and he got saved. Praise God he's saved." May I put on my pastor's hat and lovingly say, "Hold on just a minute. Not so quick. You're not done. In fact, according to God's Word, your work has just begun, my friend." Once people get saved, they need discipleship. They need somebody alongside to teach them how to walk. They need someone to care for them.

Not only did my brother play that role in my life, but God brought others as well. We have a man on staff at Calvary Chapel Fort Lauderdale named Jym Kay. He oversees our evangelism outreach ministry. He was placed in my life back in Vegas at just the right

This is me on the left, with my great friend and mentor, Jym Kay.

time. God used him as a spiritual "personal trainer." Jym was one of those seasoned saints who would challenge me to go beyond my comfort zone. He would also help me when I'd start to do dumb things. He was always ready with the Word of God to correct me.

I'll never forget one such incident. I was saved probably about four weeks or so, and I went out to try and evangelize—a fancy word for telling someone about Jesus. This may shock you because of the fact that I do it everyday of my life now, but back then, it didn't go so well. Discouraged by my failure and deceived by the devil, I ended up making a bad judgment call. I remember feeling so guilty over it that I was convinced that night that I had hurt God's feelings to such a grave degree that He had probably changed His mind about the whole grace-salvation thing. The next day, I told my brother, "Jim, I don't . . . I can't even . . . I can't even be a Christian. I can't do it. Here's what happened," and I told him the story of my failure. Jim said, "I want you to call Jym Kay on the phone." I called Jym and said, "Jym, here's what happened. I tried to evangelize and share, but it didn't work out the way I thought, and so I did something really stupid." Jym said, "Brother, listen. Don't lose it. The same grace that saved you is now the same grace that's going to sustain you and sanctify you. You stumbled, that's all, and God's grace is for those who stumble. Don't forget God's Word that says: *God is strong and can help you not to fall. He can bring you before his glory without any wrong in you and give you great joy (Jude 1:24 ICB).* With love and patience, Jym taught me these things.

As a pastor now for over two decades, I can sadly say that we don't have enough Jym Kays in the body of Christ. We don't have enough Jim Coys in the body of Christ. We don't have enough people who will see a sinner that's been touched by God and say, "I want you to come into my house and stay with me. I want to disciple you. I'll come alongside you."

This is even more regrettable when you consider in a transient community like Fort Lauderdale that people can get saved, feel the joy of Jesus, and be talking to God—maybe they're telling Him what great clouds He makes—but then they have to go right back into the pit of their old lifestyle. And when they stumble, like we all do, there's no one to help them get back up with an encouraging word from the Word.

I remember being on the phone with Jym, hanging on to every word of hope, saying, "Tell me more." He was giving me verse after verse that reassured me of my salvation. He said, "Man, God still loves you. He died for you while you were still a sinner, Bob" (Romans 5:8). As my soul and spirit began to comprehend the truth of what he was saying, I exclaimed, "While I was still a sinner, He died for me? Okay, then that must mean that He still loves me now because I don't want to sin." He led me to Romans 7 and read through the chapter with me until I said, "Okay, I think I can do this." He walked me the whole way through and concluded with, "Okay, Bob, let's ask God for forgiveness now because it says in 1 John 1:9, *If we confess our sins, He is faithful and just to forgive us our sins and to cleanse us from all unrighteousness.*"

I got off the phone, turned to my brother, and said, "Jim, I'm still saved." He said, "Well, of course you are!" I said, "Yeah, but I didn't know for sure. I mean I made a mistake and felt like maybe God didn't want me anymore, but now I know that God still loves me, and I love God all the more."

I still desperately needed discipleship. I was so ignorant of God's Word and His ways that I was saved and still selling cocaine because I honestly didn't know God wouldn't want me to make a hundred dollars for driving across the street. I seriously thought, "Hey, He must want me to make this because I tithe on it." I was in that season of ignorance that the Bible describes in the book of Romans, where my mind still needed a good deal of renewing for the work of transformation to take place: *Don't copy the behavior and customs of this world, but let God transform you into a new person by changing the way you think. Then you will know what God wants you to do, and you will know how good and pleasing and perfect his will really is (Romans 12:2 NLT).*

You have to appreciate my brother's patience. He knew what my beeper was for, and he knew it wasn't for messages. One night, I got beeped just before one of his Bible studies, and he said, "What is that for? Do you have a job interview?" I said, "No, not exactly." He knew, and I was just dumb enough to say, "No, somebody wants cocaine." He replied, "So, what are you going to do?" I started with, "Well, I'm going to . . ." and I began to get that twinge of Holy Spirit conviction, so I changed course, "I'm just going to do this last one. This'll be the last time I do this." He looked at me and said, "Last time you do it?" I said, "Yeah." Then he pressed in a bit, "Bob, come on. What are you doing?" Still in the justification mode, I said, "Well, I'll tithe it all." He said, "Bob, God doesn't need your money, and at some point in time, you're gonna to have to choose. Then you're going to have to be honest and tell these people that you don't deal drugs anymore."

Jim had the perfect balance of grace, wisdom, and correction. He would pull one of these on me all the time, "Well, go ahead. If you feel you really need to do that. Remember, now you're making decisions with Jesus. So, evidently, it's a Jesus decision. Go ahead and sell coke. And then when you come on back, we'll still have our Bible study. Or do you want to have the Bible study before you go sell cocaine?"

How do you wheedle your way around that kind

of in-your-face reality? Probably the same way I often tried, "Well, here's what I was thinking. I was thinking tonight I wouldn't have a study. That's what I was thinking." He would say, "Oh, you don't want to study with me?" to which I would reply, "Oh, no. I do want to study with you."

Needless to say, Jim eventually won out because he was there for me. But I'll never forget how it happened. One of the guys I was selling to managed a large casino. He had a huge corporate office with an oversized desk. He beeped me, and I went up to his office. I walked in, and he was on the phone, smoking one of those big cigars. He said, "Hey, Bobby, come on in and sit down. You're holding, right? You know, holding. You got some?" I said, "No, Joey, I don't." He said to the person on the phone, "Hey, hold on a second. I'll call you back. I've got to hang up." Then he turned to me and said, "What's going on? Your connection dry up?" I took a deep breath and said, "No, Joey. I gave my life to Jesus Christ, and I can't sell you cocaine anymore." He said, "What did you do? Oh, Bobby!" I repeated it again, "Listen, Joe. I-I-I-I-I can't. I gave my life to Jesus, and I can't do this anymore."

You know what he did? He sat up from his chair, he reached across the desk, and he said, "Well, I want to shake your hand." And then he shot me. No, he didn't shoot me, but he did shock me. I said, "You do? Why?" He continued, "Well, I couldn't do that Christianity, but somebody's got to be out there living it. I want you to be the man. Go out there and live it. You get out there, and you live it!"

I hope you are grasping the irony of what happened.

I was encouraged in my spiritual walk by the guy I used to sell drugs to! Can you fathom that? I walked out of that huge office feeling untouchable! I figured I could go tell the rest of the world about Jesus because Joey told me how important it was. God was even using heathens to keep me marching on, but I would not have had this experience if it had not been for the encouragement of my brother. Jim was extremely instrumental in my formative years as a believer.

There is a very bizarre ending to the story of Joey. Fast forward with me five years: I've met my wife; we're both working at Calvary Chapel Las Vegas, when one afternoon this old, beat-up Plymouth pulls in the parking lot; a frail, skeleton of a man gets out; I hear his voice in the lobby—and it's Joey. I turned, walked out in the lobby, and said, "Joey, is that you?

What are you doing here?" He said, "Bobby, I have talk to you." He walked into my office, skin and bones, shaking from drug withdrawal, and told me his sad story. He had lost his family, his position, and all his money. This guy had millions of dollars. He'd lost it all in five short years because of his sinful lifestyle.

After a few hours of ministry, I watched Joey walk off the property. While I was still contemplating the tragedy of his life, God knocked on my heart and said, "Bob, that could have been you." I acknowledged, "You're right! Oh, Lord, thank You for my salvation! Am I ever glad for Your amazing grace that saved me!"

There is an intense lesson for all of us in the story of Joey. Sometimes as Christians we may look at our circumstances and think, "I'm not satisfied with my life." Before we go there, let's consider what our life would have been like had it not been for Jesus Christ. Would I have already done your funeral? Sometimes when we wish life was a little better, I don't think we realize that it's probably only by the grace of God that it's as good as it is, but we can't always see that until we consider how much worse it would have been without Christ. What would my life look like if I had stayed on the path Joey was on?

I've been focusing on my past so that you could have a sober appreciation for why I consider my life in Christ so good. Through my testimony, I hope what you will see more than anything else is a man who is completely and totally dependent upon Jesus. When people tell me that Christianity is just a crutch for the weak, I am quick to let them know that it is much more than a crutch. On a crutch, I still have the ability to do some of the walking. Jesus is not a crutch; He's an entire hospital. I am on life support. I couldn't do anything without Him. Apart from Jesus, I've made some of the dumbest decisions I've ever made in my life. But, with Jesus Christ, I've made some wise decisions that have brought me to a place of peace and joy I never imagined possible. Becoming a Christian is all about staying connected to Christ because only in Him are we able to find the kind of life that continues to grow better and stronger day by day and bears real fruit.

Learner's Permit

Jesus said: *"Abide in Me, and I in you. As the branch cannot bear fruit of itself, unless it abides in the vine, neither can you, unless you abide in Me. I am the vine, you are the branches. He who abides in Me, and I in him, bears much fruit; for without Me you can do nothing. If anyone does not abide in Me, he is cast out as a branch and is withered; and they gather them and throw them into the fire, and they are burned. If you abide in Me, and My words abide in you, you will ask what you desire, and it shall be done for you. By this My Father is glorified, that you bear much fruit; so you will be My disciples"* (John 15:4–8 NKJV).

After that night in my brother's living room, the truth of these verses began to take root in my life. A seed of salvation had been planted, and it was beginning to grow. In the same way that a seed needs certain elements for growth, so too does our spiritual life have the same essential needs. Seeds need sunshine. Spiritually speaking, for us, that would be worship.

Through worship, we allow God's Spirit to radiate in our hearts, purging and purifying our lives. The miraculous thing about worship is that it brings the light of God to the deepest and darkest recesses of our soul. It was worship years later that first shed light on my fear of public speaking.

A seed also needs water to grow. I find it fascinating that throughout Scripture water is used symbolically for God's Word. When Jesus was talking to the woman at the well in John Chapter 4, He spoke of "living water," and Bible scholars agree that the reference is to Him, as God's Word: *Jesus replied, "If you only knew the gift God has for you and who I am, you would ask me, and I would give you living water. . . . People soon become thirsty again after drinking this water (from the well). But the water I give them takes away thirst altogether. It becomes a perpetual spring within them, giving them eternal life" (John 4:10, 13–14 NLT, parenthesis mine).*

We see this symbolic use of water for the Word again in Ephesians 5: *Husbands, love your wives, just as Christ loved the church and gave himself up for her to make her holy, cleansing her by the washing with water through the word (Ephesians 5:25–26 NIV).*

Just as a seed needs water, so we, as those who have received the seed of salvation, need the water of God's Word. In practical terms, this means Bible study. We need to dig deep into God's Word to find out His will for our lives, His heart on the issues of life, and His wisdom.

Through the light of worship, we are purified, and through the water of the Word, we have direction, but there is still another ingredient that is necessary for the healthy growth of a seed. A seed needs soil. It needs a rich and healthy environment in which to grow. For Christians, that would translate to rich and healthy fellowship with others who have also been cleansed and are growing. When we gather with other believers, we are strengthened, built up in our faith, and stirred up in our love for God. Through fellowship, we find ourselves growing in God's grace because of the fertile soil of our friends. In the safety of like-minded fellowship, our salvation can flourish and grow. Fellowship is very important, and Scripture gives us some pretty strong admonition regarding this aspect of our salvation:

The righteous should choose his friends carefully, for the way of the wicked leads them astray. (Proverbs 12:26 NKJV)

Don't team up with those who are unbelievers. How can goodness be a partner with wickedness? How can light live with darkness? What harmony can there be between Christ and the Devil? How can a believer be a partner with an unbeliever? (2 Corinthians 6:14–15 NLT)

. . . Pursue faith and love and peace, and enjoy the companionship of those who call on the Lord with pure hearts. (2 Timothy 2:22 NLT)

Soil, water, and sunshine make a seed sprout and grow, yet there is one last ingredient that catapults the growth of a seed, and a believer, like nothing else. Did you guess it? It's fertilizer. Yes, dung to be specific. When you pour on the dung, it's amazing to see how rapidly a seed grows. Now you can understand how I grew so quickly. I was enjoying amazing worship, the fellowship of my Christian friends, and a rich and deep time in the study of God's Word. And there are few soils as rich in dung as Las Vegas, Nevada.

Maybe you are experiencing sunshine, water, and great soil in your Christian walk, and maybe even a little or a lot of dung. The verses above tell us that this is all part of our Christian life. When we abide in Christ, His Spirit speaks to our hearts. We soon find ourselves able to discern the difference between right and wrong, and through the power of God's Spirit in us, we can choose to do what's right.

The Scenic Route

Through Jim's discipleship and my study of God's Word, I started to discern between right and wrong. And the Lord challenged me more and more to put feet to my faith. I remember specifically one such occasion after I had left the casino industry, while I was still staying with my brother and his wife. I was having an intimate time of worship with my headphones on, listening to a praise album. I can still remember the song, and as I sang along with the music, "Bless the Lord," God spoke to my heart.

"Hey, Bob," He said. "Yeah, Lord?" I replied. He continued, "That stereo you're listening to and singing praise songs with—that's stolen, isn't it?" I sat stunned. I didn't even know it still mattered. I responded, "Lord, I thought it was kind of given to me. I don't know if I'd call it stolen. I mean, I see it as a gift. You see it as stolen. . . ." He firmly said, "Bob," to which I replied, "Yes, Lord. Here's what I'm thinking. How could I worship You without a stereo? You want me to worship You, right? Worship's good, right? How can I worship You without a . . ." Again, I heard, "Bob" but a little more emphatically this time. Incredulous, I stammered, "Lord, You can't possibly . . . am I . . . am I . . . I'm supposed to take it back? You want me to take it back to the person I stole it from? Lord, I mean, I don't . . . I don't even know if I'd know where they . . . No, I-I guess I do know where they live."

It had been just a few months earlier that one of my friends who had a lot of property in Las Vegas was evicting a tenant, and it looked like the tenant might be fleeing his responsibility to pay rent. My friend got me on the phone and said, "Hey, Bob. What kind of stereo system do you have?" I said, "Mine's not bad." Then he set the bait, "How'd you like to get your hands on a really great stereo? I mean a real solid system." Still somewhat innocent to what was happening, I said, "Hey, man, I'd like that." He said, "Well, it's yours right now for the taking. You just have to come over to the house where I'm evicting a tenant. The guy owes me so much in back rent that this stereo is rightfully mine, and I'll give it to you." I jumped on the opportunity, "All right, John. I'll be right over."

I stashed the stuff in my car, but because my car was smaller than the stereo system, I had to strap the speakers on my roof. I made it back to my house and put the system in my bedroom at my brother's place. So, there I was, worshiping the Lord with stolen stuff, when God knocked on my heart.

I remember saying, "Lord, I know what You're asking me to do. You're asking me to call John and get the number of the guy he evicted. You know I haven't talked to John in quite a while. In fact, the last time I talked to him was when I told him about You. Now, he thinks that I am all religious and everything. Lord, this is going to be a hard thing. I know he'd probably have the phone number of the guy he evicted, and maybe with his number, I'd be able to track him down, if he left a forwarding number." This was definitely a little dung designed to let the seed of my salvation grow past the weeds of my pride.

I called my friend on the phone, "Hey, John. It's Bob. Yeah, I know we haven't talked for a while. Listen, bro. Remember that stereo you gave me? I'd like to return it. . . . Yeah, it's part of that religious thing. Yeah. Uh-huh. Can I have his number, John? Thanks. That's all I'm asking for."

I got the phone number and called it. I started out, "Hi. I know this seems strange, but I stole your stereo.

Uh-huh. Well . . . really? It wasn't yours? It was your brother's? Oh. He'll be glad it's back? Well, okay. Well, I'll bring it over. Yeah. It'll be on the front porch. Bye."

I ran it over to their house and dropped it off with a little note that said, "I became a born-again Christian. I can't have stolen stuff. Here's your stereo back."

Months went by, and I was listening to KILA, a Christian radio station in Las Vegas. During Thanksgiving, they always had a Thank-a-thon. It was kind of like a Praise-a-thon where you give funds, but in a Thank-a-thon you call up and thank the Lord for something wonderful that He's done in your life.

I was listening and thinking, "This is a great thing," when a girl came on and said, "I just want to thank the Lord for whoever it was that got saved and returned my brother's stereo. You see, he was backslidden. He had walked away from the Lord after his stereo was stolen, but he had prayed, 'Lord, if You'll bring back my stereo, I'll come back to You and begin to serve You again.'"

I listened to her testimony and had one of those God-orchestrated, Holy Ghost goose-bump moments where the hair rises on your arms, and you say, "Man, this is a very cool thing! I like this!" It was at that very moment that the Lord burned the revelation into my heart that set my course forever. He said, "Bob, when you lived for wickedness, people followed you in a wicked path. If you will live for righteousness, people will follow you on a righteous path."

I was overwhelmed with a sense of purpose and gratitude. This meant that God could actually use my life to undo some of the bad stuff I had done in the past. I got on my knees before God's throne in a faith-filled moment of hope and amazement, "Oh, Lord. I know how many hearts I've hurt. I know how many lives I've trashed. I know how many people I would disregard in my past. Do You really mean I could repair some of that?" I found out from that night forward that the answer was a resounding yes! Whenever I choose to let my life be used for the glory of God, He uses it.

This truth is not just mine, however. Romans 6 explains this scriptural principle: *Do you not know that to whom you present yourselves slaves to obey, you are that one's slaves whom you obey, whether of sin leading to death, or of obedience leading to righteousness? (Romans 6:16 NKJV)*

God is telling us that we will either be a slave to

our flesh, bearing fruits of destruction, or we will be a slave unto righteousness, bearing fruits of everlasting life. There is no such thing as a free or self-made man. Bob Dylan was right—we all serve somebody. The marvelous thing is that I realized at that point in time that I was having a lot more fun watching God work as I walked a path of righteousness than I ever did watching lives be destroyed when I had walked a path of wickedness.

If you are a believer, and you know in your heart that when you do right, God will use your life to influence others to also do right, it becomes obvious that this is one of the reasons why you received salvation in the first place and why you didn't go immediately to heaven after you accepted Christ. Have you ever thought about that?

Why don't we get taken up to heaven right after we say the sinner's prayer? "In Jesus' Name. Amen," and—poof—we vanish. That doesn't happen because we've been saved and left here to be a bright light and a path to those who might be following in our footsteps. If we choose to start swimming upstream, against the tide of popular opinion, toward the goal of the high call in Christ Jesus, we will be an inspiration to someone else to also swim upstream. Do you have any idea how vital committed Christians are in a world in which the masses are on the broad path to hell, marching their way right to eternal destruction?

Jesus said: *"Enter through the narrow gate. The road that leads to hell is a very easy road. And the gate to hell is very wide. Many people enter through that gate. But the gate that opens the way to true life is very small. And the road to true life is very hard. Only a few people find that road" (Matthew 7:13–14 ICB).*

When I read this verse, I thought, "How did those few get on that road to eternal life?" If it is so narrow and difficult to find, did God touch one person first and show him the way and the rest followed—one life at a time? The thought brought hope to my heart. "God, You could actually use my life to touch someone else's life and lead that person down that narrow pathway to eternal life."

With this revelation fresh in my spirit, I went to Calvary Chapel Las Vegas and asked how I could help or be involved. I started out in the nursery, worked my way into teaching the kids, did the Friday night gospel presentation, and then a home Bible study. God began to use my life as I laid it out for Him to use. I found that whenever I offered my life, God would always see to it that there was someone with a need I could meet. It was phenomenal. When I would meet someone's need, I experienced such unspeakable joy that I would want to meet more and more needs. I felt a sense of purpose, and I finally understood why I had been created. I no longer woke up in the morning wondering what my purpose in life was. I knew that my purpose was to give God glory in all that I did. As I made that my firm commitment, I was so satisfied personally that my joy and satisfaction were contagious. Others were drawn to me and affected by me because I was allowing God to use me for His glory. I determined in my heart that this was the road I wanted to follow forever.

When I contrasted my years before Christ to the

years after coming to know Him, I discovered an interesting fact. In my days as an unbeliever, I thought I was having a good time. And there were some parties and get-togethers where I really did have a great time. But those high-highs were heavily outweighed by some very low-lows, and whether I was high or low, my experiences failed to give purpose or meaning to my life. In contrast, my experience of salvation has defined every part of my life and even brought meaning and purpose to what I went through in my past. Walking with God has been an unbelievable venture in faith as I've watched Him redeem my past to make it something for His glory.

All-Wheel Drive

Before I give you the wrong impression, let me assure you that my life with Christ has not been smooth sailing from day one. Not at all. Remember, dung is necessary for growth, and God often uses our mistakes as the fertilizer that causes us to grow strong and healthy. The Lord knows that early on in my walk with Him, I made enough mistakes to create plenty of fertilizer.

One such mistake stemmed from my lack of really knowing God. I was volunteering at the church, and I still needed a job, so I looked for one in the record industry. I didn't think that God had the necessary connections to find me a job where I would be happy and satisfied, so I pounded the pavement in Las Vegas on my own for about a month. I remember coming home one day somewhat defeated, and my brother said, "Bob, what's going on?" I said, "Man, I've been looking for a job in the record business for the last four weeks." He said, "Let me ask you a question. Have you given it over to the Lord?"

I said, "Given it over to the Lord? Well, I've trusted God with my salvation. I know He does baptism well. I know He does communion really well. I've trusted God for all those things, you know, all the spiritual stuff. This is different, though, Jim. I need somebody with record business connections. I need somebody who knows people at the top." To my embarrassment, I went on for a few minutes expressing to him how God could probably not meet my need because it's not really anything up His alley.

My brother wisely didn't offer advice or rebuke. He simply said, "Hey, let's pray for you specifically right now." I thought, "What do I have to lose," so I said, "Okay." He said, "Now, listen. Listen to what I pray," then he grabbed my hands, and I'll never forget how specific his prayer was. "God, right now Bob is looking for a job in the record industry. You know that's what he does well. He's looking for a company car. He's looking for an expense account. You can deliver that. Thank You. In Jesus' name. Amen." That was the prayer, and Jim was very, very specific.

It was Friday afternoon, so I couldn't go out and look any more that day. I was kind of excited though to head out on Monday and see if God would answer Jim's prayer. Oh me of little faith! Don't you know, Friday afternoon I got a phone call from a sister at our church. She said, "Hey, Bob, did you see the paper?" I said, "No, I didn't see the paper." She continued, "Well, I thought I remembered that you were looking for a record industry job, and as I was looking through the classifieds, I found this ad that says, 'Looking for a record industry executive.'" I replied, "Wait a minute! I've never seen an ad like that." Then she read the ad to me, and it was just what my brother had prayed! I called the guy on Monday.

Just so you know how truly neophyte I was in the Lord, for the next two days, I set out to live a very, very holy life. I prayed, "Lord, there's a job. It might be perfect for me and . . . ." I was trying to bribe God into giving me the job! Can you believe it? I'll bet you can believe it and that you've done it as well!

When I reached the guy on Monday, he said, "I'm only in town one day. I'm looking for a sales rep that will cover the western region of the United States. Here's what the job offers and entails." Then he said, "Tell me a little bit about yourself," and after a brief discussion he told me to come down to the Frontier where he was holding interviews.

When I met with him, he asked for my resume, and after looking it over he commented, "You've got years of experience in the record industry. You are probably overqualified for this job. You are like a top promotion guy. Why wouldn't you want to pursue that field?" I decided that honesty was the best policy, so I told him, "I got tangled up in cocaine and alcohol. I can't afford to get back into the promotion side. I don't want to be around that lifestyle. I need a sales job." He said, "You're being honest." I replied, "Yes, I have to be. I gave my life to Jesus Christ, and He's changing everything around, including my integrity." He said, "You did what?" So, I repeated it, "I gave my life to Jesus Christ, and that means that I want a life of honesty and integrity." He then said, "I think you really mean that, and you've certainly got enough experience to fill the job. You've made my day a lot shorter since I only have to interview you. Can you be in Phoenix tomorrow?" I was surprised but said, "Yeah, sure I can." He finished with, "Okay then, you've got the job."

I left that interview with thoughts racing through my mind. I was processing the entire absurdity of the situation. I had searched for four weeks and could not find a connection to save my life. God found the connection on a weekend, through a friend, via an ad I never saw! I was blown away and thought, "This is an amazing thing, the way that God works!" From then on, I prayed a lot more specific prayers—"Lord, five-foot-four." No, just kidding!

The Importance of a Guardrail

I had been at the job for about year when I learned how deceitful our flesh can truly be. I was enjoying the work and doing well at it, but I was really loving the time I spent volunteering in ministry more. So, I thought, "I know what I can do. Since I have the job down pretty well, I'll spend a little more time at church and just fudge over here on some of my reports so that it won't be that noticeable. It seemed innocent because my heart sincerely desired to do more and more ministry.

Unfortunately, it was at the expense of integrity. It wasn't long before the same guy that had looked at me at the beginning of my tenure with the company and said, "Hey, you are really a go-getter," was now sitting me down and saying, "Wait a second. What are you doing with these accounts? It looks like you're stuffing product here and doing something not so kosher there."

It's the trap in which many Christians can naively find themselves. I wanted to do full-time ministry so badly that I was forsaking the responsibilities to my employer in the process. I'm telling this part of my story specifically for those of you who are reading this book right now and aspiring to a ministry position. Here's what you may be erroneously assuming: "Well, even though I haven't been that faithful in this or that vocation, now that I'm saved, I'll be a faithful minister for God." I hate to pop your bubble, but that's not how it works. The Bible gives very keen insight into God's heart on this matter when it says: *"The master was full of praise. 'Well done, my good and faithful servant. You have been faithful in handling this small amount, so now I will give you many more responsibilities. Let's celebrate together!"* (Matthew 25:21 NLT)

God rewards our faithfulness in small things with the responsibilities of greater things. We also see in Scripture that He considers those responsibilities concerning the Kingdom to be of more importance than those in our earthly life and thus requiring an even greater degree of trust: *And if you are untrustworthy about worldly wealth, who will trust you with the true riches of heaven? (Luke 16:11 NLT)*

Until you've been faithful with your responsibilities in the temporal world, God is not going to entrust you with privileges in the spiritual world. God does not reward slothfulness. Instead, He admonishes us: *Slaves (or employees, in our cultural timeframe), obey your masters (employers) in all things. Do not obey just when they are watching you, to gain their favor. But serve them honestly, because you respect the Lord. In all the work you are doing, work the best you can. Work as if you were working for the Lord, not for men. Remember that you will receive your reward from the Lord, which he promised to his people. You are serving the Lord Christ (Colossians 3:22–24 ICB, parentheses are mine).*

There is a secondary reason God will not reward your unprofitable behavior in a secular job. When you are working in the ministry, you are still dealing with people from the secular world. What kind of a witness would it be if when others ask you how you decided to go into the ministry, you say, "Well, it was an easy decision. I started shirking my responsibilities in my worldly job and became a total mess-up at my workplace, so my boss fired me, and now I'm working for God." I don't think so! That is not a testimony that would glorify the Lord in the least. That's why God had to send an associate pastor to set me straight.

Pastor John at Calvary Chapel Las Vegas had seen me hanging around the church probably a little more than he thought was normal for someone who was employed full-time elsewhere. He approached me and said, "Hey, Bob, listen. I see you drive a company car, and you're hanging around here at the church a lot helping out, which we really appreciate. I also noticed that you're sporting a pretty decent tan, so I was just wondering, when do you work that job that provides the company car?" Being absolutely clueless, I said, "Well, it's really cool, John. I mean, the way God worked it out for me, I'm able to just balance it out." He then said, "Well, as long as you're not ripping off your employer. I mean, if he expects forty hours, you ought to give him forty hours." A little embarrassed, I admitted, "Well, no, he actually expects like fifty-five hours, and I think I may be giving him thirty and just squeaking by at that." The truth of his words had such an impact on me that I went back to my job the following day and determined in my heart to start serving my boss like I was serving the Lord.

An amazing thing happened once I started doing business as though I was serving God. I discovered that when we simply do what our employer expects of us, we become promotion material. We stand out from the rest of the world because most folks are not doing what they're called to do. They're performing barely sub-par work. In fact, they are barely accomplishing the requirements of the job. They just squeak by every day at their workplace thinking, "I'm sure if my boss could find somebody that works a little bit better than me, he would, but he probably can't because everyone else is like me, so I'm pretty safe."

When we become one of those rare people who go beyond what we're called to do, who are not like the sub-par people just squeaking by, and who actually do some things that we're not even asked to do, we shine like a bright light. That's when we enter real ministry because we have stepped up to the plate that Jesus has set for us to glorify God: *"Let your light so shine before men, that they may see your good works and glorify your Father in heaven"* (Matthew 5:16 NKJV).

That's what happened to me. I started working for God in my secular job, doing above and beyond the call of duty. My sales figures skyrocketed, and it was all because of my honesty and integrity. It was at this point that God knocked on my heart to do full-time ministry. I was so busy working for Him at my job that I was a little taken back, "Wait a minute! You want to call me out of the business world now when I'm being successful?" The answer was emphatic, "Yes, Bob, exactly."

It's not hard to convince people to go into ministry when they have been a miserable failure in business. That's about the time they are looking for any form of escape. Ministry looks great in comparison to misery. But that's not what God wants to do in their life. He wants them to rise to the challenge of proving themselves in the secular world before taking on spiritual things. Then, when somebody asks, "Well, how did you end up in ministry?" the story will reflect the glory of God.

I am so thankful that God did not let me get into the ministry the way I was heading. It is comforting to know that if someone questioned my work ethic, I could gladly say, "Please, check with my boss, and he will tell you that before I left and started working for Calvary Chapel Las Vegas I had a very good business reputation." That is so much better than if I had actually filled out an application at Calvary Chapel Las Vegas and someone there had called my previous boss to ask, "I'm curious. What is Bob's work ethic? He has filled out an application to come on staff at the church, and I just want to know what kind of job he did for you." They would have heard massive laughter and a response that went something like, "Well, hey, he should be on staff there. He doesn't work around here! He spends more time at your church hanging around than he ever spends here working. So, great, I'll fire him, and you can have him. I don't even mind helping to pay for him to get into the ministry since he is really worthless around here."

That's sad and sick, and that's why I'm grateful that God didn't allow it to go down that way. I am sorry to say that after twenty-some years in the ministry now, I have found that in too many circles of life Christians have a terrible reputation in their workplace. They have made the notion of a Christian worker an oxymoron. Let's not have them say, "Christian worker? They work? I thought they just talked about Jesus all day. I'm shocked at the idea that they work."

I know we are given the Great Commission by Jesus to share our faith, but it should be on our time and dime, not our employer's. I made that mistake myself. I was talking about Jesus during my on hours and actually thinking that He was blessing me because I was bringing people out to my car and sharing a tape, "Hey, you want to hear this Dr. Walter Martin tape? Hey, how about a Chuck Smith tape?" God has called us to be a witness of His excellence and integrity, not a slouch who steals time from his or her employer to talk about God. I had learned that lesson the hard way, and now I was ready for ministry.

Back on Track

I was in Phoenix at a meeting with all of our sales representatives from across the United States. I watched my boss, Tom, as he laid out on a graph all of our sales for the prior year. He said, "And now, here's where we've got Nick." We were looking at Nick's sales, which are kind of up and down, when Tom said, "But here's Bob. Now take a look at Bob's sales. Bob, I don't know what you're doing here, buddy, but your sales are skyrocketing." Tom didn't realize it, but I knew that, because my head was on straight and God was giving me wisdom, peace, power, and favor, I was doing really, really well as a businessman.

The sales numbers would have been the only thing that mattered to me before, but now there was something more glaring than the graphs. Something else was going on in my heart that stemmed from my connection to Christ. I found myself more interested in the people than the profits. I knew Tom well enough to know that he had recently left his wife and that he was an alcoholic. And while he was praising me in front of all my peers, I was lifting up an urgent and silent prayer, "God, please use my life to reach Tom. I don't care about sales. I care about Tom's salvation!"

I don't know if it's happened to you yet, where you find yourself at work saying, "This is really wonderful, but where is the eternal value in what I'm doing?" That's where I was. I was thinking, "Sure, I got great sales. Yeah, okay. Wonderful. But it isn't enough anymore. I can't keep on doing this." So, I made the decision to leave my great job in the record business because I wanted to serve at my church full-time.

Two weeks after that meeting, I said to Tom, "Tom, I'm giving you my notice. I can't stay here. The whole time you were talking about the sales, I couldn't stop thinking about what is going on in your life. I'm more interested in your heart than I am in how much money you are paying me." He seemed a bit uncomfortable. "Well, Bob, I'm really glad you're interested in my life, but that's a little personal," he said. I knew I had to press in, so I did, "Well, Tom, everyone knows you're an alcoholic and you left your wife. It's not like you're hiding it. You've been pretty open about it. I really want to talk to you about those things." We had a very decent dialogue, and towards the end of the conversation, he said, "I can't lose you. How about if I give you the state of Hawaii? How'd you like to oversee Hawaii?"

It was like the devil was taunting me with the ultimate territory, "Come on, Bob. Hawaii! Forget ministry. No salvations for you, buddy! Just lots of money and perks. Come on. Sales, buddy, sales!" The devil must have forgotten that I'd been there, done that, and had found it pathetically deficient to meet the real needs of my heart. I said, "No, thank you, Tom. Hawaii and sales aren't going to do it for me." He reminded me, "Bobby. You've got a brand-new color television set in the mail. You hit the goal last month. Think about what you're giving up." I responded, "I know the job has wonderful benefits and privileges, but I really want to go into ministry. You deserve a sales rep that's with you eighty hours a week. I know that's what this job demands, and I can't do that anymore. I want to start serving at my church."

The On-Ramp to Ministry

I left that meeting a little nervous because I was well aware that I was giving up quite a bit of security and prestige. I had opted to take a job at a store called Montgomery Ward in the TV department. It was not a great career move, but the hours that I would be at work did not interfere with the hours I wanted to volunteer at the church. The job afforded me plenty of time for ministry, and that was my main priority. I had made the connection for this job through someone I used to sell records to, but when I got to work the first day in my suit and tie, the woman in personnel said, "You better go talk to the manager up there in the TV department."

The manager then informed me, "Bob, I can't hire

you." I said, "Can't hire me? I just left a job and said goodbye to my company car because you said I had a job with you. I drove here in a borrowed vehicle. What are you doing?" He said, "I'm really sorry. I had hired you to replace a woman who has been with us for some time. She just changed her mind, and now I need to hire her back because she knows the product better than you. I sure feel bad about this, but I hope you understand."

What I understood was that I was out of a job and in a borrowed car. I thought, "Lord! What am I going to do?" I hopped into my borrowed car and drove to the church because I felt such a strong impulse to pray. I went into the building and knelt down to be alone with God, hoping to get a clue as to what might be happening.

Right about that time, one of the pastors came walking down the stairway from the second floor, and when he saw me, he asked, "Hey Bob, what are you doing here?" I said, "Well, I just lost my job." He said, "Yeah, but I thought you were leaving that job?" I said, "Yeah, I left the job I had, and I got another job, but I just lost that job." He got a funny look on his face and said, "Well, why don't we go get some lunch." I was game for that since I figured that he could help me sort through my future career choices.

We went to McDonald's, and I as I sat there having lunch with the pastor I couldn't stop smiling inside as I contrasted that picture with all the power lunches I had been to in my life. I had dined and discussed business at some of the most impressive restaurants in the country with some of the richest people in the

world. Now, I found myself sitting with a relatively unknown individual at a non-descript, everyman's chain restaurant. Yet, in hindsight, that lunch at McDonald's turned out to be one of the most powerful lunches of my life.

While we were eating, the pastor said, "What do you see in your future?" I didn't even have to think about it. I responded, "I'd love to minister full-time. If I could just work for God, it would be so fantastic. I don't even need that much money because my expenses are really low." He asked, "Could you make it on three hundred bucks a month?" I thought maybe I had heard him incorrectly, so I said, "Three hundred bucks a month?" He said, "Yeah." I thought to myself, "I make more than that in a week! Is this really ministry?" Then my wheels started spinning out loud.

"Okay," I said, "Well, let me see. I'm paying $225 a month for my apartment because I'm sharing it with a guy, and I don't really have many other expenses. Yeah, I think I could do it on $300 a month. I would just need a vehicle." He said that wouldn't be a problem, so I took the job.

I had not been working at Calvary Chapel Las Vegas long when my need for a vehicle became pressing. The pastor had promised me a car, and I was meeting him to look at it when I remembered a statement I had made to God back when I was still an unbeliever. It was one of those things you say when you don't really know God. I said, "God, listen. I might someday get serious about You, but here's what I'm not going to do. I'm not going to wear an old pair of jeans, a T-shirt, love beads, and drive a '65 Chevy with bumper stickers on the back. Okay? There are just some things I'm not going to do."

As I look back at it now, I think this aversion probably stemmed from the stereotypical Christian that I seemed to always encounter, those Jesus-freak types that would walk around in a non-real world saying, "Oh, hey, man. God loves you." I could never understand why someone couldn't just be a Christian business person. It seemed like all the Christians I came across were losers and destitute. It had actually made me wonder if it was considered sinful in the Christian faith to have things, like possessions, or a brain, for that matter. I always wrestled with that because I didn't identify with that mindset at all. I don't think most unchurched people do identify. It wasn't until I saw my brother's conversion that this stereotype got shattered.

The reason I had this flashback about my statement with God was because as the pastor walked me out behind the church building, what do you think awaited me as my new company car? You guessed it—the '65 Chevy with Christian bumper stickers all over it! I was laughing to myself as I thought, "Lord, You definitely have a sense of humor."

I think the more astounding part of this story was not that God gave me the car I said I would never drive, but that it really didn't matter to me what I was driving. I was just so happy to be serving in the ministry. This transformation was an amazing testimony to the work God had done in my heart. Before coming to Christ I had always been extremely prideful about the kind of car I drove. Yet, none of those cars or any other possession I attained in the world before accepting Jesus could hold a candle to the joy that God gave me as I drove that '65 Chevy all around Las Vegas serving Him. Jesus said: *"For even I, the Son of Man, came here not to be served but to serve others, and to give my life as a ransom for many" (Mark 10:45 NLT).* I was happy to accept the humble status of a servant because that's Who my Savior is.

One Way

ROAD WORK AHEAD

CHAPTER 3

Jym Kay had so successfully nurtured me back to faith through that first botched attempt at evangelism that we soon became witnessing warriors together. I loved seeing lives changed through the gospel, and I still do.

Proceeding with Caution

My pastor at Calvary Chapel had seen me with Jym on the strip in Vegas telling people about Jesus. He came to me at one point and said, "Bob, I'd like to see you share the gospel some time after a Friday night movie or a concert." I got really excited and said, "Man, that would be great!" He said, "Why don't you come up and do the announcements this week on Sunday morning? That will give you a feel for speaking from the pulpit. You can get used to it, and then next Friday night you can do the gospel presentation after the movie night." I said, "Okay, let's do that."

That next Sunday morning, he said to the congregation, "And now Bob's going to come up and do the announcements." I was standing in the back of the room, and when I heard him say that, my heart started palpitating. My underarms started perspiring. My mouth went dry, but I knew where all the water went because it was pouring out the palms of my hands. I got halfway down the aisle and decided, "I can't do it." I grabbed the announcements, turned to an associate pastor, and said, "You've got to do this. I can't do this," and I bolted out the door. I ran all the way to the drinking fountain and stuck my mouth by the spout for about five minutes. I wasn't drinking, mind you, I just wanted to get moisture on my tongue.

After the service my pastor found me and asked, "What happened to the announcements, Bob?" I was painstakingly honest with him and said, "I don't know. I was just scared to death. I don't think I can talk in front of people." He simply looked at me and said, "We'll see."

For those who are familiar with the ministry of Calvary Chapel Fort Lauderdale, it might shock you to read this. It is easy to assume that because I get up in front of approximately 18,000 people every week, and over 20,000 people at our Christmas and Easter services, that I have always been adept at public speaking, but as you can see, that is simply not the case.

It wasn't long before the pastor asked me to speak again. This time he wanted me to give the altar call after our movie night. I sensed it was the Lord's will for me to take the challenge, so I got on my face in my living room and prayed in earnest. I knew that in order to do what God was asking of me, I was going to need His strength to do it. In that time with God, I had an intense time of worship to a Keith Green song. The lyrics jumped out at me like the voice of God:

God's calling, and you're the one

But like Jonah you run

He's told you to speak

But you keep holding it in,

Oh can't you see it's such a sin?

The world is sleeping in the dark

That the church just can't fight

Cause it's asleep in the light

How can you be so dead

When you've been so well fed?

Jesus rose from the grave

And you, you can't even get out of bed.

Oh, Jesus rose from the dead

Come on, get out of your bed.[1]

It was right then that I had my "Garden of Gethsemane" moment. It became a "not-my-will-but-Yours-be-done" defining experience in my life. I left that prayer time with the commitment that if I died presenting the gospel at the movie night, at least I would enter heaven seeing a smile on God's face.

I sat through the entire movie with a knot bigger

than Texas in my stomach. When the movie ended, I reluctantly but obediently stepped up and took the microphone, which I held tightly against my lips so the people could not see them twitching. If that wasn't bad enough, only a few minutes into it, I realized I would have to sit down because my knees were knocking so hard from fright I thought I was going to fall over. Through all of this, I continued to just share the words God was giving me, although I was pretty sure that no one would even listen, let alone respond at the end.

As I got close to the conclusion of the invitation, I decided to turn my back to the audience to avoid the humiliation of no one coming forward. I told them that I was going to kneel at the altar, and they could come up to pray with me if they wanted to accept

Christ. You can't even begin to imagine my shock when I realized that people were coming forward and kneeling next to me. In spite of my twitching lips, knocking knees, and lack of faith, God orchestrated Kingdom business through a fearful but willing vessel.

My pastor was such an encouragement to me. He asked me to take the next Friday night, and I did. Then he asked me to take the next Friday night, and I did again. I just kept doing the Friday night thing, and through that experience I overcame my fear of public speaking and learned to exercise the gift of teaching that God had given me.

Now, you can see why I tell you this story. I wouldn't want the fact that today I speak to thousands of people on a weekly basis make you assume that it has always been something I've been comfortable with. My comfort today is nothing short of a miracle. By the grace of God, I teach six services every week now and have been doing that for years, but know this: I am every bit as dependent upon God for my ability to do this as I had to be that very first time I shared the gospel after the movie night at Calvary Chapel Las Vegas.

I am revealing this part of my life for that one person who will read this book and realize that God can use anyone. As it has been well said before, "God does not call the qualified, He qualifies the called." I was called, not qualified, so God gets the glory for all that has happened in my life since that first movie night at Calvary Chapel Las Vegas. It's not about what a great, confident speaker I am but about how desperately I still have to rely upon the grace of God to

do what He calls me to do. I think the Lord actually calls those who aren't very qualified so that He can fully get the credit for what He does through them. That was the point the apostle Paul made: *Brothers, look at what you were when God called you. Not many of you were wise in the way the world judges wisdom. Not many of you had great influence. Not many of you came from important families. But God chose the foolish things of the world to shame the wise. He chose the weak things of the world to shame the strong (1 Corinthians 1:26-27 ICB).*

Mistaking the Road Signs

Another thing I had to learn as a new Christian was how to have righteous relationships. I remember the first Christian girl I dated. She was so spiritual that when she prayed, I thought I saw angels right above her head. I was convinced that she was the one for me because she didn't swear and she loved her mom. To me that was like, "Wow! I met a girl who doesn't swear and loves her mother. This is unusual. She must be my wife. This is great."

Then I started hanging around the church, and I found out that there were lots of women who didn't swear and loved their moms. It was an eye opener for me to see just how inept I was at handling this part of my life. Ironically, even though I realized I knew literally nothing about choosing a wife, I still seemed to be insistent upon keeping this part of my life within my own control.

There are a lot of singles who come into our church at Calvary Chapel Fort Lauderdale and think,

"Hey, this is church? How many Bible studies do you have a week? I'd like to be a part of this fellowship." They say that because they see all these beautiful, godly women and wonderful, godly men and think that this is a good place to meet their match. On the one hand, it is; but on the other hand, it's not. I warn them to be careful because God knows our motivation. More than that, He also knows our morality. I've warned the guys in our church that every single lady is a daughter of God. If their intentions are not pure and holy towards her, they better be ready for God to start working on their own morality issues.

It's not that God is against us meeting our mate. In fact, marriage was His design in the first place. God wants singles to have a relationship, but He wants them to have one that is birthed by His Spirit.

What He doesn't want is for His people to engage in relationships that are so self-centered, shallow, and futile that they are no different than the ones they had before they knew Jesus. He wants their entire relationship—from start to finish—to be spiritually strong and rooted in the knowledge of Christ. That's the lesson that I had to learn.

I had only dated this Christian woman for a few days, but I thought she was my wife. We truly did have some fun and special times together. I remember turning to her and saying, "Look at how our relationship is developing and how things are going. This must mean that God has intended us to be together." I honestly believed that the will of God would be established in just studying the Word with each other, singing some songs, and attending Christian functions together.

The interesting part of all this is that every one of these ingredients will happen in a God-willed relationship, but they are not what makes it God's will. There are many wonderful Christian men and women with whom we can enjoy all these things in the arena of friendship without it being any more serious than that.

I talk to couples from time to time who start making more of their relationship than they should based solely upon these criteria. They come in, and the guy says, "Hey, I found my woman." So, I'll ask, "Well, how do you know?" to which he replies, "Well, man, when we study the Word, it's great. And when we sing songs together, it's like heaven. And we love to go out and witness together." Again, these are all wonderful things, but they can happen with anyone—that's Basic Christianity 101. It doesn't mean that the person is your mate. God looks at much more than the basics in determining what His best is for you. He is looking far into your future and wants to bring you a partner that will fulfill His long-term vision for your life. He's not into the short-term "wow-we-get-along-really-great-and-she's-hot" model of dating. He has long-haul criteria that involve things on a higher plane.

As we move away from the purely physical and mental components that we built our relationships in the world upon, we will enter into the emotional and spiritual aspects of a relationship that constitute the highest plane of compatibility. It is at this level that we find a match that can endure twenty, forty, sixty, and even more years.

That was one of the reasons God had brought my first Christian girlfriend into my life. She was a true woman of God who was only interested in the spiritual. Her commitment was so established and strong that I actually felt like I was on holy ground around her. The thought of kissing her never even entered my mind. For the many months I dated her, I actually thought if I kissed her, my lips would burn off or I'd break out with leprosy or something like that. I had a very keen awareness that she was God's daughter, so I stayed far away from any physical involvement with her.

This is a great lesson for all the single girls who are reading my testimony. Your commitment to Christ can keep many a young man from making a wrong move. Your commitment protects not just you, but the guy as well.

I did learn a lot from that first relationship about what a spiritual relationship should be. It taught me how important self-control was in my own life. This was very important for the next girl that I dated because she was a little bit more into the physical than the spiritual. With what I had learned in my first relationship, I was able to be the strong person in that second relationship so that we never crossed a line that would offend God. As weird as it was for me, I had already seen the wisdom of waiting in my first relationship, so when she made her advances, I was able to say no. I knew by now that to pursue the physical end of the relationship was not the best way for us to honor one another and God.

Before I met my wife, Diane, God allowed me to spend time with four different women who taught me a lot about myself and about the Lord. The reason I bother to tell you this is because I never found myself in a physical relationship with any of these women. That is why we were always able to maintain our spiritual relationship at the highest level and why to this day I still have good friendships with each one of them. Our relationships lasted beyond the dating period because they were friendly but not fleshly.

As much as I thought each one was supposed to become my wife, I had to start looking past my own thoughts and tapping into God's discernment to make that critical decision.

The Emergency Brake

This discernment was honed on my fourth relationship. Of all the women I had dated to that point, I was the most certain that she was the right one. She was attractive, had a bouncy personality, and was always in a great mood. She loved the Lord. She was perfect in every way, except for one. She didn't have a pastor's wife's heart.

The amazing thing about it is that I didn't even know that was a prerequisite, but God knew the future He had planned for me, and He knew what I needed. I needed a woman who could have a heart for the ministry more than for herself. She would have to be sacrificial in this department if she was to serve alongside me in my calling as a pastor.

Don't get me wrong, she was a great girl. I met her parents, and she met Jim and Theresa. Everybody really liked her, including me. That's why I could not figure out for the life of me why there was something in my heart that just kept saying, "No." It was like I couldn't get the emergency brake to release so I could go forward. I remember asking the Lord, "What's wrong? Everything seems so good." The Lord quietly impressed on my heart, "Watch her in ministry, Bob."

I was involved in teaching Sunday school at the time and would also share at the singles' Bible study, so I had several opportunities to observe her in ministry. As I began to pay more attention to detail, I noticed that her heart wasn't interested in other people as much as it was interested in me. It was great that she was devoted to me, but I needed more than that. I needed to know that I would have the freedom to minister without the pressure of keeping her company. She tended to resent the time that I gave to the ministry. I could tell that no matter how perfect it seemed to be, the relationship wouldn't work out in the long run because I was being drawn more and more into ministry life.

KEEP
RIGHT
CHAPTER 4

As much as I wanted to get married, that experience with girl number four kind of blew me out of the water, so I decided to put the whole relationship thing on hold.

A Matrimonial Merge

I was talking to a friend about my decision, and he said, "Well, Bob, why don't you do this—since you obviously don't have the gift of celibacy, it is safe to assume that you will eventually be married. In order to keep from being preoccupied with who you're going to marry, why don't you just start praying for the person that God has for you and wait for her."

I thought, "You know, that's a good idea." So, I started praying for her, and I even remember my prayer:

"Lord, I don't know who she is, but I know she's living. I know she's alive right now. I know she's somewhere on this earth. So, Lord . . . ," and I continued on with many different requests for my future wife.

I was still praying for her when the Lord knocked on my heart one night and said, "Pray for her salvation." I stopped short and said incredulously, "Lord, she's not saved yet?" He just repeated the instruction, "Pray for her salvation," so I started praying for her salvation.

Months passed after that night of prayer, and I was working at Calvary Chapel Las Vegas, enjoying a time of serving God full-volume in ministry. I was so busy, I remember ironing, getting lunch, getting dinner, and saying in a kind of "side-note" type of prayer, "God, I need a helper. You know, as in 'help mate'? A helper like You gave Adam."

This is the beautiful woman I fell in love with back then and whom I am privileged to be married to today.

One afternoon, there was a knock on my office door. I was sitting at my desk, and I looked up and saw two girls and a guy walk in with my pastor. I thought, "Wow, that blonde is the most beautiful woman I think I have ever seen. What a bummer. I'll bet she's married to the guy." Right about then my pastor said, "Hey, Bob. Did you meet Diane and Lori?" I said, "No, I haven't yet." He informed me, "The girls are here from Calvary Chapel West Covina to serve for the next week. Can I put you in charge of their responsibilities while they're here?" I replied, "Sure. I have no problem with that. What do you want them to do? Do you want them involved just in ministries that I oversee or in all the other ministries as well?" He said, "It doesn't matter. Just keep them busy for a week. They have hearts of servants, so let them dig in wherever there is a need." I found out quickly that the blonde—Diane—was not married to the guy.

I had grown enough in my relationship with Christ to know that next to accepting Him, the most important decision we will ever make in our life is who we choose as a spouse. Since my track record of picking women was so bad, I had made kind of a deal with God. I had prayed, "God, I want You to bring me Your choice of mate for my life. And here's how I'll know that she's Your choice: if she loves You more than I love You, I'll know she's Your pick for me because I know how much I love You. But I want her to love You more than I love You. I want her to love You more than she'd ever love me. That's what I'm looking for."

That happened to be Diane's heart. She came to Calvary Chapel Las Vegas with such a servant's heart that as she was busy about her work, she wasn't paying any attention to me at all. I actually got a little offended because I was doing everything to get her attention. I was telling jokes. I was boasting a little, telling her, "Hey, I teach Sunday school. The kids love me. I'm great with kids." Nothing. I couldn't budge her attention in my direction no matter what ploy I pulled out of the hat.

Her mind and focus were so much on the Lord that I couldn't distract her. I even invited her to a barbecue at my house that turned out to be just Rod, a friend of mine, Diane, Lori, and me. Not as big a barbecue as she had thought. To this day, she laughs about how I tricked her. She'll tell you, "I thought there was going to be a pile of people over at Bob's

I can't believe the actual grill we barbecued on over twenty years ago is still there, but it is, and this is it!

house. When Lori and I got there, it was just Bob and Rod." We did have a great time, though. We barbecued, watched a Christian video, and worshiped the Lord. For me, it was a special time of getting to see her heart in a social setting.

She continued to serve the Lord, and I noticed that she and I got along really well, and the friendship began to build. Near the end of the time that she was serving at the church, I said, "Can I pray with you for a minute before you leave?" She said, "Yeah, sure, what's up?"

Because she was everything I was looking for in a wife, after just four days I looked her in the eyes and said, "I'd be willing to wait twenty years for you. You're an incredible woman." She stared at me like I was crazy. But no matter how crazy she thought I was, when she went back to California we started to communicate long distance. Over the next eight months, we built a solid, spiritual relationship—mainly because we couldn't do anything else! She was three hundred miles away! God knew exactly what He was doing.

Through the distance, everything was about the Bible. And it was really good because God knows me so well. He says, "You really want her, don't you? Okay. Watch this. You will prove your love by waiting—for her and for Me."

I had that opportunity to prove my love, and here's the beautiful thing that happened. God gave me a single mind toward service to Him because I had already decided in my heart that Diane was going to be my wife. I was not distracted by any of the single girls that came to the church because that decision had been made. It was wonderful. I was able to serve God with a complete heart but at the same time be devoted to Diane.

Diane already had that single focus toward God and stayed busy in California devotedly serving Jesus. In hindsight, I should have invested in AT&T when she went back to California because I spent hundreds of dollars on the phone talking long distance. I don't regret a minute or dollar of it, though, because all those conversations—when we talked about the Word, prayed together, shared devotions with each other, and discussed what God was doing in her life and in mine—were worth their weight in gold. They established a solid foundation, one we would need sooner than later.

This is the second best decision
I ever made in my life.
The first was accepting Jesus
who gave me this beautiful bride.

After eight months, she made the decision to move to Las Vegas. We dated for another eight months before we got married on November 17, 1984.

When we were on our honeymoon, we started talking about how unlikely it was that we had even met. For Diane to have ended up at Calvary Chapel Las Vegas when she really would have preferred to go to Villa Vicencio, Colombia, to volunteer for that week was nothing short of God's hand at work between us. During the course of the conversation, it occurred to me how glad I was that she was saved and sitting with me as my wife. When I told her that, she said it was even a miracle that she was saved because she didn't know anyone who had been praying for her to get saved. That's when it dawned on me that I was the one who had prayed for her salvation. How thankful I still am today that I hadn't questioned God the night He told me to pray for my future wife's salvation.

Traveling Mercies

Now, some people have said to me, "Well, wait a minute. You just said that you were married before, but you're a pastor. How do you reconcile that with God's Word that says a pastor should be the husband of one wife?

I reconcile it with God's Word, which says that: *If anyone belongs to Christ, then he is made new. The old things have gone; everything is made new! (2 Corinthians 5:17 ICB)* If you remember my story, my first wife said I had to be "born again" to be with her, so I prayed an obligatory prayer for her sake. It didn't take, as my life revealed afterwards. I gave my heart to her, not Jesus. But, in the living room of my brother's house on Christmas night in 1980, I did become "born again." I was made new, and the old—including my three-week marriage was gone.

From that moment, I maintained personal purity until I met and married Diane. I believe that in those waiting years, God restored my mind when it came to the physical dynamics of a relationship, but I also believe He did one other thing that only He could do, from a spiritual perspective. He made me a new creation in Christ. He restored me to a place where, when I pledged my life to Diane that day at Calvary Chapel Las Vegas and said, "I want you to be my wife," I came to her pure, holy, and chaste.

Morally and spiritually, we started our relationship fresh and new. The evidence of this miracle is that over the last twenty-plus years that we have been married God has made certain that our relationship did not suffer the consequences of our past, but continues to receive the blessings of our future. What God has done is nothing short of a miracle.

The Exit Ramp

One afternoon, after six months of marriage, before our move to Fort Lauderdale, Diane said to me, "Bob, what do you think about this church here at Calvary Chapel Las Vegas?" I said, "Why do you say that?" She said, "I'm not sure why, but something feels wrong." That feeling turned out to be valid discernment. I am sad to say, but the church that I was first a part of in Las Vegas got very weird. I'm only telling you this because there are valuable lessons for all of us in the body of Christ that came out of the unfortunate decline of that church.

Many people have watched Calvary Chapel Fort Lauderdale grow and could rightly have some of the same fears that I have, "Will the success go to my head?" Hopefully, I have gained the benefit of wisdom at the expense of what happened at Calvary Chapel Las Vegas.

As that church started to grow, the success began to affect the heart and head of our senior pastor. It started out with subtle changes like renaming the church. I couldn't pinpoint that alone and say it was wrong, but I knew, at least in my heart, something was off. I also became aware of a lot of decisions the pastor was making apart from his board of directors. A man with a successful ministry but without accountability is a scary combination. He also had authority over the finances of the church. These were all very, very dangerous practices and attitudes that eventually led to the church's downfall. The church eventually disbanded altogether. But God kept His promise to work all things together for good (Romans 8:28), and now Las Vegas is the home of several solid Calvary Chapels. One of them, in fact, is led by an assistant pastor from the original staff.

When someone comes to me today and says, "Hey, I noticed that we are doing more television and radio outreach. Is Calvary Chapel Fort Lauderdale going to be like those other churches that just get into television ministry and forget the individuals within the four walls of the building?" I can assure them that that's not our focus. I have already gleaned the benefit of seeing where that leads, and I can earnestly say that I loathe the idea of becoming someone who sees himself as a success story. What I see as the success story in this congregation is the success of Almighty God flowing through ordinary people. I pray constantly that we never find ourselves with such a high and lofty head, in some way assuming that we had something to do with the grace of God. I am deeply aware that I personally have had nothing to do with the success of this ministry. I attribute it solely to the grace of God. I can't improve on His righteousness, so why would I for a moment, in an attitude of arrogance, think that God's grace is because of me?

In a very strange and divine way, it was our growing apprehension about Calvary Chapel Las Vegas that caused Diane and me to decide that we needed to seek

God for another direction. We began to pray and consider where God would lead us. Diane shared her heart with me and said, "You know, Bob, I've always thought that the best place for a Calvary Chapel would be where there isn't one. I really have a heart to see a Calvary Chapel on the East Coast." As I considered her suggestion, I replied, "Well, the East Coast doesn't have very many Calvary Chapels at all." In fact, at that point in time, there was only one other Calvary Chapel in the entire state of Florida. There are many more now, but Merritt Island was the only place that had a Calvary Chapel back in 1985. Diane said, "Well, then, let's pray about the East Coast." I said, "Okay," and we continued to pray.

The custom at Calvary Chapel Las Vegas was for people with prayer needs to fill out prayer request cards and drop them in the tithe buckets when they went to church. At 6:00 a.m. every weekday, those interested in praying for the needs of the church would meet together and pray over the cards that had been collected.

One morning, I ended up with a prayer request in my hand from a couple in our church that was moving to Fort Lauderdale, Florida. The prayer request read, "We're moving to Fort Lauderdale, Florida, or at least Coral Springs, and we want to pray that God raises up a Calvary Chapel pastor that would start a church there like this one here." It was my turn to pray, so I said, "Lord, we're lifting up the Carters. They are looking for a Calvary Chapel in Fort Lauderdale. Lord, I pray right now that You would lift up a pastor for Calvary Chapel Fort Lauderdale. Lord, bless that man with a vision for Fort Lauderdale."

The strangest thing happened as I prayed that prayer. It was as if the words were leaving my mouth and entering my own heart. I couldn't get them out of my heart and head. They were like glue to me.

After the meeting, I was walking out in the courtyard when the wife of the couple who submitted that prayer request came up to me. She said, "Hey, thanks so much for praying that prayer for the Calvary Chapel Fort Lauderdale. Hey, maybe you're the pastor for that Calvary Chapel! Ha, ha, ha, ha." There was nothing unusual about how she said what she said, but there was definitely something different about how I heard it. I heard it echoing through my soul—"Maybe, maybe, maybe . . . you're, you're, you're . . . the Calvary, Calvary . . . Chapel, Chapel . . .

pastor, pastor, pastor." It was as if she had shouted it from one of the loudest megaphones on earth throughout the entire universe. I was actually starting to think, "Wow, maybe I am!"

When I got back home, I said to Diane, "You are not going to believe what just happened. I prayed today for a Calvary Chapel church plant in Fort Lauderdale. What do you think?"

You have to know this was totally God because I was not familiar with Fort Lauderdale at all. I had been there once before in my life for a week when I graduated from high school. We were partying so much that I honestly don't remember any of it. That's why when Diane said, "Well, have you ever been there?" I had to admit, "I was there once, and I have a T-shirt, but I don't even remember where I bought the

T-shirt." I know that was not much help, so she just said, "Okay, well, let's start praying about Fort Lauderdale." So, we started praying.

Two nights later, Diane and I went out for ice cream and stumbled across a travel agency that had a map of the United States in the window. I said, "Well, let's take a look at where Fort Lauderdale is anyway. Let's see, here's Vegas, and Fort Lauderdale is over . . . oh, it's over . . . Diane, it's near Cuba! That's where it is. It's right next to Cuba!"

It seemed really far away. The next thought I had was about Diane's parents. They lived in California. Then, I realized, "This is going to be a hard thing for her to adjust to. She's going to be three thousand miles away from her mom and dad."

Right at that moment, her precious ministry

heart spoke up, "Bob, whatever the Lord is speaking to your heart, I'm behind you one hundred percent. If He says Fort Lauderdale, I'm ready to go." With that kind of trust, I knew we needed to be sure that it was God and not Bob, so I said, "Diane, you pray, and I'll pray. Let's find out what God says. If He says 'Go', we'll go."

I know that God knew we were serious about the sacrifice, so He came through in an unmistakable way. Diane had a girlfriend that worked with her in the bookstore at Calvary Chapel Las Vegas. They were really close friends. One day, shortly after we had started praying for Fort Lauderdale, her friend called her and said, "Diane, I've been praying and fasting." Now, Diane and I had also been praying and fasting because we really wanted to hear the voice of the

Lord. We had not told a single soul what we were praying about. We didn't want a lot of opinions; we only wanted direction from God. Her friend continued, "Are you and Bob moving to Fort Lauderdale, Florida, to start a church?" Diane was in shock, "How do you . . . ? We haven't told anyone! Not even the pastors know!" Her friend explained, "Well, the Lord just spoke to my heart, and I thought He said Fort Lauderdale. Are you guys leaving?"

Diane was so excited to tell me about this amazing confirmation, but we both agreed that we still wanted the Lord to continue to speak to us so that we could be completely sure. I prayed and said, "Lord, it seems that You want us in Fort Lauderdale. If You can keep on speaking this way, we'll know."

For the next few days, everywhere I went in traffic

I kept seeing Florida license plates. I introduced myself to a vendor in our bookstore, and I asked, "So, where do you live?" Yes, you guessed it—"Well, we live in Fort Lauderdale, Florida" was the reply.

It began to get ridiculous. Wherever we went, we were running into something that screamed Fort Lauderdale. Every time we opened God's Word, we got another confirmation. Finally, after a week, I said to Diane, "Honey, I think we need to start packing up the truck." She agreed, and we began to prepare for our departure.

Yes, We're There

I had been teaching a Sunday afternoon service at the church. There were probably a couple hundred people who attended. When I made the announcement that we were moving to Fort Lauderdale to start a Calvary Chapel, all of a sudden people came out of the woodwork to tell us, "We're coming with you. We're going to be by your side." We had volunteers for worship leaders, children's ministry—you name it.

I had to say, "Wait a second. This is the vision the Lord has given to me and my wife. I am not expecting others to jump on board here unless they hear from God themselves." I actually had to start discouraging people from coming with us, and with the exception of one family, I succeeded.

I knew Fidel and Theresa Gomez and their family pretty well. Fidel was serving as a deacon at Calvary Chapel Las Vegas. He called me about three weeks after I had made the announcement and said, "Bob, a strange thing happened. My wife and I were praying, and we feel called to Fort Lauderdale to help you start that church."

I really tried to discourage Fidel because he had three small children. I didn't want anyone to distract me or get in the way of God's plans for my life. So, I said some pretty bold things to him like, "Fidel, you guys can come, but you have to get there on your own, and I can't be responsible for you when we arrive. I also cannot be slowed down by anything." He didn't seem phased, so I turned up the heat.

"In fact, Fidel, I'm going to tell you something. You know your little son, Gabriel? Well, let's say this. Let's say we get to Texas, and he gets terribly ill, and you have to put him in a hospital in Dallas. I'm going to keep on driving to Fort Lauderdale at that point, Fidel. Do you understand how critical it is that I get to

Fort Lauderdale?"

I know Fidel a lot better now. He served with me for five years, then pastored his own church, and is now back with me as an assistant pastor. I wouldn't even try to talk him out of anything today because I know how stubborn he is in pursuing God's call in his own life. That day, he set his face like flint and said, "Bob, if my son gets sick in Dallas, you go on. Once he gets out, I'll be back in the truck and on my way to Fort Lauderdale."

Two days before we were ready to leave, Fidel called and said, "Hey, have you got one truck or two trucks? Do you want to share?" I said, "You're really going, aren't you?" He answered, "I'm really going." "Well, then, if you're really going, we might as well go together," I concluded.

That top picture is Calvary Chapel Las Vegas
praying for our trip to Fort Lauderdale,
the next two are Diane and I,
together with Fidel and Theresa Gomez,
the couple who came with us across the country
to start Calvary Chapel Fort Lauderdale,
packing up the U-Haul for our venture in faith.

We drove all the way across the United States. We didn't even know what we were doing. When we finally hit Florida, we got on the turnpike heading south toward Fort Lauderdale. When I saw the first Fort Lauderdale exit sign, I pulled over to the side of the road, got out of the car, and said, "Fidel, we made it to Fort Lauderdale!" He said, "We made it!" We ran toward each other—you can imagine it in slow motion with background music—I hugged him, he hugged me, we sat down, and I looked at him and said again, "Man, we made it! We made it! It's been one long week, but we made it." Then he asked a question I'll never forget. He said, "What do we do now?" That's when it dawned on me that I had not even thought that far ahead. I said, "I don't know. What do we do now? I have no idea what we're supposed to do."

NO **U**
TURN

CHAPTER 5

Now that we had made it to Fort Lauderdale, I really didn't know what to do next. I said, "Well, let's head toward the beach. I like the beach." So, we started driving down Commercial Boulevard for the very first time, wondering where we were going to live.

Which Way Do We Turn?

We got a room at a tiny hotel on the Galt Ocean Mile. Later, when we were behind the building doing our laundry, we encountered Florida's state bird—the mosquito! The next morning, my legs, my back, my face—everything was swollen. We were feeling pretty forlorn as we soaked in the pool to make the swelling go down from all our mosquito bites.

Then, I looked out over the ocean, and there was

a huge rainbow. I sighed and said, "Yes, Lord, I remember Your promise. You really do want me here, don't You? Do You? Don't You? Do You? Don't You?" (Can I tell you that wrestle went on for two years? For two long years, I wasn't sure if I was really supposed to be in Fort Lauderdale.)

While we were in that hotel for a week, I was crying out to God, "Lord, where do You want me to live? I'm spending rent money on a hotel room."

God led us to an apartment just off Commercial Boulevard, two blocks down from Floranada Elementary School, where the church would eventually meet. For the next three weeks, we looked for regular jobs and held church in Fidel's living room. Then we found a funeral home that let us hold our church services on Sunday mornings. Finally, we had saved

These two pictures show
God's faithful provision
in the apartment He provided for us (top)
as He was having our house built (bottom).

enough nickels and dimes to move out of our apartment and purchase a small house nearby, around Commercial Boulevard and Andrews Avenue. On the day of our closing, as I was signing the deed, I noticed the date the house had been built, and it hit me like a ton of bricks. It was built the same month in 1985 when we had driven down Commercial Boulevard on our first day in Florida and wondered where we were going to live. I didn't know back then, but God did. He had it all planned. We had to live in an apartment for three years because God was building us a house.

Unfamiliar Territory

If you look at the history of Calvary Chapel Fort Lauderdale, it seems absolutely foolish to the natural mind that a church that started in a living room, then

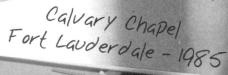

Calvary Chapel
Fort Lauderdale - 1985

This is one of our early church services
that we held in Fidel and Theresa's living room.
The guy on the left playing guitar is Rod Pearcy,
my roommate back in Las Vegas,
who now works as my ministry assistant
here in Fort Lauderdale.

moved to a funeral home, was pastored by a guy who had no formal training in theology, and without a real worship leader, could ever make it off the ground. Can you even fathom inviting someone to come to your church at a funeral home? Or how about having people come and listen to a worship leader who taught himself how to play four chords on the guitar on the trip out from Las Vegas to Florida. Those early days were amazing testimonies to God's power and grace.

I remember sitting in the back of the funeral home on Sundays, behind a curtain where they kept the caskets, and looking out at Fidel playing the guitar. His eyes were so glued on the chords and what he was playing that I was sure he couldn't really be entering into worship. I'd peek out from behind that big curtain and think, "Lord, are we ever going to have real church? Ever?"

One afternoon, I finally turned to Fidel and said, "Fidel, here's what you have to do. Get your eyes off the neck of the guitar. I want you to close your eyes. I want you to focus on the Lord."

About three Sundays later, I was sitting in the back as usual, and suddenly I heard him just worshiping the Lord. I thought, "Man, this sounds great!" I looked out, and there he was with his eyes closed, just singing songs to the Lord. He'd mastered those four chords well enough that he could make the transition from chord to chord without looking at his fingers.

Now, I need to add one more bit of information to this picture. Fidel used to sway back and forth while he worshiped. So, while I was watching him and thinking how great he sounded and how in the throne room of God he was, I noticed that he was swaying. He kept swaying and turning until I thought, "He's turning around! He's got his back to the crowd!" And Fidel had his eyes closed, so he didn't even know he had his back to the congregation. I looked out at the people in the church service, and they were elbowing one another and giggling, but Fidel was having the greatest time just worshiping God.

That's some of what would happen in those early days. We went through a lot of growing pains, many of which left us laughing until our sides ached, and many of which left us deeply wounded. Yet, through all of it, God was orchestrating His plan for Calvary Chapel Fort Lauderdale.

Roadside Assistance

We were in the ministry in Fort Lauderdale about a year and a half, and we had a get-together for the church over at a place called Whirly Ball. They had little go-carts that you could get in and drive around as you tried to hit a little ball. It was a total riot.

We were there to just have some fun, but before the meeting got underway, I asked everybody from the church to hold hands in the middle of the Whirly Ball court and pray. Just as we were about to begin, I noticed this kid who worked there who was kind of hanging around. It was his job to make sure that the go-carts were working right. I said, "Hey, you want to pray with us?" Caught a little off guard, he said, "Uh, yeah, sure." He took hold of our hands, and in a somewhat condescending way, he prayed with us.

Then he went into the back and started making pizzas for the night.

It got to be around 10:30 or 11:00 p.m., and they were closing up the Whirly Ball court for the night. We were saying goodbye to all the folks from the church. We were the last ones to leave because we were paying the bill.

Unexpectedly, from out of the back, this kid called me, "Hey, Preacher! Hey, man! Mister!" I said, "Yeah." He said, "Hey, could I talk to you for a minute?" I said, "Sure, what's on your mind?"

I felt like the apostle Paul. It was a scene straight out of the Philippian jail. The kid says, "Ah . . . I just want to talk to you about this Jesus. I mean, how do you get saved?" By the grace of God, I recovered pretty quickly from my shock, and I said, "You want to get saved? Hold on one minute. I'll be right back!" I turned around to find Diane who was waiting for me outside. She had overheard the conversation. She looked at me and said, "Go, go!" waving me on like my final lap at the Indianapolis 500.

I went back inside where he was still making pizzas. They had closed the Whirly Ball but were still selling pizzas for carry-out. I always get such a chuckle out of God using my assorted and distorted background for His glorious purposes. I had worked before in a pizza place, so I started chopping onions and helping him make the pies. He and I began talking, and, slowly but surely in the course of two and a half hours, this guy finally got to a place where he said, "I'd like to open my heart and receive Christ." So, I prayed with him to receive the Lord. Then, we closed up the restaurant together.

I was walking out of the kitchen when it suddenly dawned on me that I had left my wife in the front of this place. She had been sitting there for two and a half hours. I could only imagine what was awaiting me when I got around the corner! I walked up to her and began immediately apologizing, "Oh, Diane. I'm so, so sorry."

You want to hear a ministry heart? She said, "No! Don't be sorry. I peeked in and saw you guys talking. I've been out here praying that he would receive Jesus." Can I just say that this would not have been the reaction of girlfriend number four to being left out in the dark alone for that many hours?

And God knew that. He knew I could never pastor a church like Calvary Chapel Fort

Lauderdale with a wife that would question my every sacrifice. It wouldn't work with a woman who would always be asking, "Well, how late are you going to have to be at church?" or "What do you mean two Bible studies on Wednesday night? I want you home by nine."

After our Wednesday night services now, I typically get home around 1:00–1:30 a.m. When I walk through the door, Diane is usually waiting up and wanting to know how it went. Some nights, I'll call and say, "I may be really late. I just wanted to tell you goodnight in case you want to head to bed early." She will often say, "No, I'll be waiting. What do you want to eat when you come home? You want chicken soup and a sandwich?"

The Road Forks

My test in faithfulness to the ministry hit after one and a half years. Although we had some really wonderful people attend the church who were very, very faithful (some of them are still with us today), the size of our fellowship at that time was only about forty people. I was getting really discouraged. The group I had ministered to in Las Vegas was much larger.

About this same time, I started getting calls from the people in Las Vegas. "Bob, do you want to come back? Oh, Bob, why don't you come out here and start a church?" It was very tempting. Everyone in Las Vegas already knew who I was, whereas in Fort Lauderdale, it seemed like I was always having to tear down walls of unfamiliarity. I had to continuously assure people in the congregation, "No, you can trust me. Yes, I'm going to be here."

Diane and I used to call them "Lookie-Lous." They'd come into the church, not really ready to stay. They were just looking. And they always had their comments afterwards, "Here's what I think about the worship; here's what I think about the building; here's what I think about your outfit, etc. . . ." Every week I would listen to five or six people say, "If you want your church to work, I think you ought to . . . ." I knew what I was called to do, but I had to listen to opinion after opinion after opinion.

Finally, the temptation to leave was just too strong. I called the guy at Calvary Chapel Costa Mesa who oversees all Calvary Chapels and said, "Listen, Las Vegas is asking me to come back. You know what happened to the church. They need a pastor, and I only have about forty to fifty people here in Fort Lauderdale. I'm thinking I should go home. What do you think?"

The guy listened to my sob story and then said, "Bob, I think you should go." I said, "What do you mean?" He said, "Well, if you don't want to be in Fort Lauderdale, God's not going to make you stay there. He doesn't want you sulking around Fort Lauderdale, saying, 'Oh, I have to take care of forty people in the church.'" Then he dropped the bomb, "You know what, Bob? Go back to Las Vegas. I have several young pastors here at the Bible College. They'd love to go out to Florida and care for those forty people. They would do that in a second."

His response wasn't quite what I had expected to

hear. I thought I was going to get one of those "Battle Hymn of the Republic" speeches. You know, "Come on, Bob. You can do it! You may be feeling weary, but hang in there, bro! You can do it." That's not at all what I got. I got truth thrown in my face, "You don't want to minister in Fort Lauderdale? Go wherever you want to go, but don't think you're going to be a burden to the Lord."

I chewed on this tough piece of counsel for a couple of days, and then one day I was driving down the expressway, somewhat depressed. I was having a conversation with God that went something like this, "Lord, I've got this flock. I've been here two years, and there are only forty to fifty people. I don't know what to do."

I was tuning my radio dial when suddenly I heard

a voice that sounded familiar. As I listened, I finally recognized that it was Greg Laurie.

Greg is the senior pastor of a Calvary Chapel called Harvest Christian Fellowship in Riverside, California. I have always had an incredible admiration and respect for Greg. One reason is because we share a similar style of teaching. Greg shares biblical truth, but he also has a sense of humor. In fact, in my early years as a believer, it was Greg who influenced me. As I would listen to his teachings, I thought, "There are a lot of people who can relate to a guy like this. There needs to be more people in the pulpit like this man." His teachings had an incredible impact on my life.

So, when I was scanning the radio dial and heard Greg's voice, he had my full attention. I don't remember the exact words he used, but the gist of what he said was, "A lot of you are looking at where you are right now and saying, 'Hey, do I really belong here?' Well, why don't you just bloom where you're planted? Why are you always looking on the other side of the fence? Don't you think God can use you right where you're at?"

He had hit the target so hard on the head that I had to pull over to the side of the road because I was beginning to have one of those burning-bush experiences. I got out of my car, walked over to the place where you could jump off and die, and just stood there. I'm sure a lot of people driving by were thinking, "This guy's going to jump." That's not at all what was happening in my heart. I was saying, "Lord, You're testing me. You want to see if I'm going to stay. So, here's what I'm going to tell You today. Starting right now, these will be my streets, and these will be my people. I'm staying here whether the church grows or not. God, I believe You can make me bloom right where I'm planted."

I got back in my car, drove home, and knew that something major had taken place, although I would not see the full measure of that transaction until several years later. However, the next week the church doubled in size and has been growing ever since.

In retrospect, I had been engaged in a standoff with God for two years. I was saying to Him, "God, come on! Deliver." And He was looking down at my heart and saying, "Bob, you deliver. I'm looking for faithfulness. I'm not looking for somebody who wants to be famous."

God knew that I had a misconception about what

He had done through Pastor Chuck Smith, the founder of the Calvary Chapel movement. I had thought that if I just hung up a Calvary Chapel sign in Fort Lauderdale, I would have a couple thousand people in no time at all. God knew that I had not learned the lessons He had to teach Pastor Chuck before He could flow through him. Pastor Chuck probably heard some of the same things I was hearing from God—challenges that cut right to the core. "Well, Bob, what if you don't have thousands of people? What if you have only fifty people here for the next twenty to thirty years? Would you still be faithful to those fifty people? What about ten to twenty people?" It was like the Abraham-God conversation from Genesis Chapter 18 in reverse. Once God brought me to a place where I was mature enough to be a true shepherd and not a hireling, that's when the

ministry began to grow.

No U Turn

Epilogue

Some of you reading this testimony may have serious doubts whether God could or would do anything in your life like He has done in Diane's and mine. May I lovingly say that your doubts are completely unfounded? God never wants us to doubt His intentions. Listen to His heart as revealed in His Word:

You (God) made all the delicate, inner parts of my body and knit me together in my mother's womb. Thank you for making me so wonderfully complex! Your workmanship is marvelous—and how well I know it. You watched me as I was being formed in utter seclusion, as I was woven together in the dark of the womb. You saw me before I was born. Every day of my life was recorded in your book. Every moment was laid out before a single day had passed. How precious are your thoughts about me, O God! They are innumerable! I can't even count them; they outnumber the grains of sand! (Psalms 139:13-18 NLT)

"For I know the plans I have for you," says the LORD. "They are plans for good and not for disaster, to give you a future and a hope." (Jeremiah 29:11 NLT)

God has made us what we are. In Christ Jesus, God made us new people so that we would do good works. God had planned in advance those good works for us. He had planned for us to live our lives doing them. (Ephesians 2:10 ICB)

The Bible also tells us: *And they have defeated him (Satan) because of the blood of the Lamb and because of their testimony. And they were not afraid to die. (Revelation 12:11 NLT)*

It is my prayer that God will use the words of my testimony to defeat the lies of the enemy in your life. No matter what you have done or haven't done, who you are or who you aren't, what's happening or what isn't happening in your life, God has a plan to bless you. Please take Him up on the offer. You won't be disappointed that you did.

Part of God's plan for your life includes salvation. God would love to come alongside you and say, "If you open up your heart, I've got a gift for you." The Bible represents this gift as "indescribable" (2 Corinthians 9:15 NKJV), yet most of the message of the New Testament is the testimony of people like you and me trying to describe this amazing thing called salvation. Without salvation, none of the rest of God's plan for your life is possible. Salvation is the door we all must walk through in order to lay hold of the eternal life that God has for us.

We can go through life fulfilling our own purposes and plans and doing our own thing, but when we get to the end of this life, we will still have to answer to God. The Bible says: *God raised Christ to the highest place. God made the name of Christ greater than every other name. God wants every knee to bow to Jesus—everyone in heaven, on earth, and under the earth. Everyone will say, "Jesus Christ is Lord" and bring glory to God the Father (Philippians 2:9–11 ICB).*

In other words, it is God's will for all human beings to submit to the plan He has for them in Christ Jesus. Someday, God will ask each of us, "What did you do with My Son? Did you accept My gift of eternal life through Him and live in the plan He had for your life?" It will be very sad for those who have to answer, "No, Lord. I didn't accept Your gift."

Maybe you think you aren't good enough for God to use you. You may need to go back and re-read this book. Remember, all I did was open my heart to Jesus Christ. I didn't have seminary or business degrees. I was lost as a rock, addicted to cocaine, a self-centered womanizer, and a man-pleaser. Yet, all I did was open my heart!

If right now you will open your heart and say, "Okay. If God can do that in Bob's life, I will also give Him my open heart and see what He has in store for me," trust me, He'll blow your mind. Every morning that I get up and race into my children's rooms, look into their eyes, and contemplate what God has given to me, I still sense my total unworthiness for such blessings. Every weekend that I pull onto our church property, I am absolutely awestruck that anyone would wake up on a Sunday morning and come to hear what I have to say about God. So many Sundays before service, I have spent on my face on the floor of my office crying out to God, still trying to understand why He would use a sinner like me to save souls. Though I don't understand, I am overwhelmed with the joy and gratitude of having opened my heart that Christmas night in 1980 at my brother's house. It is why I say to you now, "Open your heart and let Him bless you as He has blessed me and so many others."

God doesn't play favorites. He is willing to work in anyone's life who is open and ready. We simply need to position ourselves in that place of a humble heart, recognizing that His love and grace are sufficient to transform our lives and touch the rest of the world through us. He doesn't call the qualified, He qualifies those called who will be bold enough to walk on the narrow path of one surrendered life.

Prayer

Perhaps, as you have read through this book, you've felt a longing to let go in total surrender to the Lord. That longing is God's Spirit prompting you to let Him take control and orchestrate His plan for your life instead of your own plan. If you're ready, just pray the following prayer from your heart, and your adventure in faith will begin.

God, I realize that I have been trying to do life on my own, but now I want to surrender my life to you. I know you have a great plan for me. Please forgive me for the sins and mistakes I have made apart from You. I acknowledge that You sent Jesus to suffer and die on the cross to pay the penalty for my sins. As He rose again on the third day, He conquered hell and death and is now offering me eternal life through His finished work. *I accept Your precious gift of salvation. I open my heart today, and I invite You inside to be my God, to be my Savior, and to be my Friend. Forgive me of my sins, wash me clean, for I have decided this day to follow You, Jesus. From this day forever, I'm Yours. In Jesus' name I pray. Amen.*

Notes

[1] "Asleep in the Light," written by Keith Green. ©Birdwing Music/BMG Songs/Ears to Hear Music (Admin. by EMI CMG) All rights reserved. Used by permission.

Resources

Want to find out what the Lord is doing through one surrendered life?

You can access all of Pastor Bob's teaching messages by logging on to www.activeword.org.